RELEN✝LESS
LOVE

RELENTLESS LOVE

God's Faithfulness in the Face of Human Failure

LISA HARPER

Our purpose at Howard Publishing is to:

- *Increase faith* in the hearts of growing Christians
- *Inspire holiness* in the lives of believers
- *Instill hope* in the hearts of struggling people everywhere

Because He's coming again!

Relentless Love
© 2002 by Lisa Harper
All rights reserved. Printed in the United States of America

Published by Howard Publishing Co., Inc.
3117 North 7th Street, West Monroe, Louisiana 71291-2227

05 06 07 08 09 10 11   10 9 8 7 6 5 4 3 2

Edited by Michele Buckingham
Interior design by John Luke
Cover design by LinDee Loveland

Harper, Lisa, 1963–
    Relentless love : God's faithfulness in the face of human failure / Lisa Harper.
        p. cm.
    Includes bibliographical references.
    ISBN 1-58229-250-7
    1. God—Love. I. Title.

BT140 .H37 2002
231'.6—dc21

2002068568

Scripture quotations are taken from the HOLY BIBLE, NEW INTERNATIONAL VERSION®. Copyright © 1973, 1978, 1984 by International Bible Society. Used by permission of Zondervan Publishing House.

to my
friends
and
family

You've listened to me more than anyone should have to!
And you've loved me better than I ever expected.

Special thanks to my pastors:
Dr. Charles McGowan and Roy Carter.
Charles, your steadfast, Christlike love for your "sheep" has
encouraged my heart more than you know. And Roy, thank you for
being a walking, talking textbook on leadership…and for tutoring
me in all things Hebrew!

CONTENTS

Introduction 1

Chapter 1: adulterated affections 7

Chapter 2: struggling with sovereignty 19

Chapter 3: the necessity of neediness 33

Chapter 4: problems with perception 47

Chapter 5: faltering forefathers 61

Chapter 6: the perils of pretense 77

Chapter 7: bargain-basement grace 93

Chapter 8: company that corrupts 107

contents

Chapter 9: really big rocks 123

Chapter 10: misunderstanding majesty 137

Chapter 11: balking behind barriers. 153

Chapter 12: the mark of maturity 165

Notes 177

INTRODUCTION

Teresa Moshell, one of my closest friends, bounced into my office one morning, giggling as she set her guitar down. She'd just gotten back from a visit to a tiny southern town, and she couldn't wait to share one of the colorful slices of small-town life she'd been privy to!

Teresa met a woman in the town who had rounded up her entire family to attend their church social. When the youngest son, Jimmy, announced that he wanted to sing a solo in the program, the woman was thrilled, assuming that her five-year-old wanted to sing the "B-I-B-L-E" song they'd been practicing at home. She beamed when Jimmy's turn came, and he bounded onto the stage and grabbed the microphone. But her pride turned to horror when her strong-willed son shattered the sanctity of the Southern Baptist shindig by belting out the raucous lyrics to the Hank Williams Jr. song "A Country Boy Can Survive." If you haven't heard this "classic" in a while, one of the more memorable lines is:

> We make our own whiskey and our own smoke, too,
> Ain't too many things these 'ole boys can't do...

We grow good 'ole tomatoes and homemade wine
And a country boy can survive.

Instead of sweetly singing a Bible camp song, her mischievous kindergartener had cleared his throat and burst forth in a ribald tune about cigarettes and beer!

Teresa and I got so tickled that morning talking about all the ways children embarrass and disappoint their parents, especially in "religious" settings! Because even mild-mannered children don't always behave appropriately in church or in front of our "church friends." And some parents get really bent out of shape about it—as if their spiritual reputation is somehow dependent upon what pops out of their offsprings' mouths or how much the kids fidget in the pew on Sunday.

Our conversation reminded me of how very different our heavenly Father's character is. Every single one of His children has rebelled in some way or another. We've thrown temper tantrums, shoving our fists in His holy face and arrogantly demanding that the King of Kings give us different circumstances. We often misbehave like strong-willed kindergartners, too, determined to do whatever we want.

Throughout history God's people have wandered in literal and figurative deserts, searching in all the wrong places for something to quench our thirsty souls. "Looking for Love in All the Wrong Places" is another cheesy country song with significant spiritual application! We're a ragtag crew of reprobates who get it wrong far more often than we get it right. But the great news of the Gospel is that in spite of our flaws, God is faithful. In spite of our mistakes, He extends mercy.

Recently my friend Teresa and I have spent more time crying

than laughing. She's walking through a very difficult, very sad situation that involves some Christian friends who can't admit they've made a mistake. And their pride has inflicted much more pain than they realize. Yet in the midst of her disappointment and hurt, I've watched Teresa respond with humility and kindness. I think it's because she's so keenly aware of her own propensity to sin—and therefore, her need for God's mercy—that she's able to extend more compassion to others. Even when their sin stabs her right through the heart.

Teresa's seemingly irrational, loving response to a bunch of Benedict Arnolds reminds me of the woman who washed Jesus' feet with her tears, dried them with her hair, and then anointed those feet that would soon be pierced on a cross with expensive perfume. The Pharisees were appalled at her lavish, "inappropriate" behavior. It just didn't make sense to them. But Jesus said this woman loved lavishly because she had been forgiven lavishly. Her poignant display of adoration reflected her gratitude for His grace. That woman (who is referred to as a "sinner" in Luke 7:39) and my friend Teresa (who is usually referred to as "a gifted Christian singer and song-writer") have much in common. They both recognize their own depravity and their desperate need for God.

This book is about human failure and God's faithfulness. It's about our never-ending need for our Father's compassion. It's about the divine mercy He extends in spite of our mistakes. The mercy He extends in spite of our doubts. Its message is meant to encourage everyone honest enough to admit they aren't perfect. There is hope—because there is a Redeemer whose love for us isn't bound by our behavior.

Whose love for us isn't deterred or swayed by our imperfections.

Whose love for us is positively *relentless*.

We may run from His mercy and hide from His grace, thinking, *How could God possibly love someone like me?* But the truth is, God is faithful even when we aren't. Hopefully the following pages will remind you of that.

He is pursuing us at this very moment with His amazing love. Are you ready to be found?

The bromides, platitudes, and exhortations to trust God from nominal believers who have never visited the valley of desolation are not only useless; they are textbook illustrations of unmitigated gall. Only someone who has been there, who has drunk the dregs of our cup of pain, who has experienced the existential loneliness and alienation of the human condition, dares whisper the name of the Holy to our unspeakable distress. Only that witness is credible; only that love is believable.

—Brennan Manning

chapter one

ADULTERATED
AFFECTIONS

It's been a red-letter weekend for me. I've had two dates with two different men (which is cause for great celebration among my friends and family). Sometimes months go by with no dates, so to have two in less than forty-eight hours is quite extraordinary.

Come to think of it, dating itself is quite extraordinary, especially for those of us closer to forty than twenty. For one thing, our bodies begin to send messages—subtle at first and then much louder—that gravity is not our friend. I never dreamt in my svelte twenties that I'd wear the kinds of restraining undergarments I wear now. They're called "body shapers" or "body smoothers." But a more apt description would be "breath killers," because it's difficult to inhale and exhale when you've got python panties squeezing your tummy in.

It's amazing what we go through to appeal to the opposite sex. And while we know that the size of our stomachs isn't nearly as important as the size of our hearts, we still secretly pine for the type of romantic physical attraction that will take our breath away, leave us weak in the knees, and cause us to see stars (which actually describes how I felt on my dates this weekend, thanks to my desperate "squeezation" measures!).

I think most of us at some time or another dream of having a love relationship the way it's depicted in the movies—the way Humphrey Bogart loved Lauren Bacall, Spencer Tracy loved Katherine Hepburn, or Richard Gere loved Julia Roberts. Do you remember *Pretty Woman*? It was one of the highest-grossing romantic comedies in movie history, and it's still on a lot of "best movie" rental lists. I'm certainly not advocating or condoning the morality—or lack thereof—in that film; but I do think it's an unbelievably romantic love story. Julia Roberts plays the gorgeous, good-natured prostitute opposite Richard Gere's harried, hard-hearted businessman. To make a long story short, Richard—a very handsome, very successful corporate hotshot—asks Julia—a cute, naive call girl—to masquerade as his date at a few important social soirees. After spending some quality time with her (not to mention lots of money on her "makeover") he falls madly in love with her, despite the fact that she sells her body for money.

I cried at the end the first time I watched *Pretty Woman*, because I was so moved by the amazing love the two characters had developed for one another—a love that made the mountain of differences between them melt away. I wanted to be "Julia" (the *pursued* part—not the *prostitute* part!) and I wanted to find my "Richard"!

Do you still sometimes find yourself wishing that you were someone's "Cinderella" and that you could find your "Prince Charming"?

Now that I'm a little older, I'm not quite as emotionally affected by their love affair. And I find myself questioning the believability of the plot. I've decided that a love story like *Pretty Woman* is pretty unrealistic. Since Richard Gere portrays a man who could have any woman he wanted, why in the world would he settle for a streetwalker? The story line just doesn't make sense. Yet interestingly enough, it parallels a true story nestled in the pages of the Old Testament.

Wayward Wife, Scattered Sheep

Open your Bible to about two-thirds from the front, and you'll find the true tale about a man named Hosea and a woman named Gomer, who was a prostitute. (I've always wondered if Gomer slept with so many men because she had deep-seated insecurities about her name. I apologize to any of you whose mother saddled you with the same moniker!) In Hosea 1:2–3 we read: "When the LORD began to speak through Hosea, the LORD said to him, 'Go, take to yourself an adulterous wife and children of unfaithfulness, because the land is guilty of the vilest adultery in departing from the LORD.' So he married Gomer daughter of Diblaim, and she conceived and bore him a son."

It's difficult at first to understand why God would tell Hosea—a sincere prophet of the Lord—to marry a woman who was and would continue to be unfaithful to him. Can you imagine God telling you that the person you were going to fall in love with and marry was going to rip your heart out? But the truth is, God sovereignly chose to use Hosea's marriage to Gomer as a tangible, living example of His "marriage" to His people. God used Gomer's unfaithfulness to Hosea to illustrate His people's unfaithfulness to Him. The whole thing begins to make more sense when we read what Hosea named their children (and you thought *Gomer* was bad!):

Then the LORD said to Hosea, "Call him Jezreel, because I will soon punish the house of Jehu for the massacre at Jezreel, and I will put an end to the kingdom of Israel. In that day I will break Israel's bow in the Valley of Jezreel."

Gomer conceived again and gave birth to a daughter. Then the LORD said to Hosea, "Call her Lo-Ruhamah, for I will no longer show love to the house of Israel, that I should at all forgive them."

After she had weaned Lo-Ruhamah, Gomer had another son. Then the Lord said, "Call him Lo-Ammi, for you are not my people, and I am not your God." (Hosea 1:4–6, 8–9)

I'm the first to admit that the names of Hosea and Gomer's children are very strange. I doubt you'll find them in any of those books listing ideas for baby names. However, those ancient names were very significant; because in the original language of this text (Hebrew), they prophetically described what had happened between God and His beloved people. The first son's name, *Jezreel*, means "scattered"; the daughter's name, *Lo-Ruhamah*, means "no more mercy"; and the youngest son's name, *Lo-Ammi*, means "not mine." We can only imagine how that last little boy's name must've pierced Hosea's heart. The baby didn't look the least bit like him, and Gomer probably had no idea which barfly was his biological father. She'd slept with too many men to keep track.

And oh how those names accurately describe the tragic, tattered relationship that God had with His people. He had rescued them from slavery, provided food and direction in the desert, destroyed their enemies, and delivered them into the Promised Land. He had never left them or forsaken them. But they'd definitely left Him. Like Gomer, Hosea's wandering bride, God's people had become infatuated with other "lovers." They worshiped false gods, poured their energy into practicing idolatry, and betrayed their one true love, the Lover of their Souls. As a result of their spiritual "adultery," they were now scattered like sheep without a shepherd, no longer experiencing the mercy or fatherhood of God.

Have you ever felt emotionally scattered because you weren't focused on your relationship with God? Do you feel spiritually "focused" now?

Portraits of Mercy

Frederick Buechner paints a great picture of Hosea and Gomer's marred relationship—and thus God and His people's—in his book *Peculiar Treasures*. He writes:

She was always good company—a little heavy with the lipstick maybe, a little less than choosy about men and booze, a little loud, but great at a party and always good for a laugh. Then the prophet Hosea came along wearing a sandwich board that read "The End Is at Hand" on one side and "Watch Out" on the other.

The first time he asked her to marry him, she thought he was kidding. The second time she knew he was serious but thought he was crazy. The third time she said yes. He wasn't exactly a swinger, but he had a kind face, and he was generous, and he wasn't all that much crazier than everybody else. Besides, any fool could see he loved her.

Give or take a little, she even loved him back for awhile, and they had three children whom Hosea named with queer names like Not-pitied-for-God-will-no-longer-pity-Israel-now-that-it's-gone-to-the-dogs, so that every time the roll was called at school, Hosea would be scoring a prophetic bull's-eye in absentia. But everybody could see the marriage wasn't going to last, and it didn't.

While Hosea was off hitting the sawdust trail, Gomer took

to hitting as many night spots as she could squeeze into a night, and any resemblance between her next batch of children and Hosea was purely coincidental. It almost killed him, of course.[1]

Gomer's (and Israel's) adultery is defined in Hosea 2; my friend's wife's adultery was defined by her car in another man's driveway. My friend saw the car very early one morning after doubting his wife's story that she was visiting an old girlfriend from college. He said he felt sick to his stomach when he realized that her car sitting there meant that she was asleep inside the house, lying in another man's arms. He soon found out that she'd been having an ongoing affair. I asked him recently why he was willing to take her back after all she'd put him through—all the lies, the humiliation, the betrayal. And he simply said, "I love her. And the promise I made to her was sacred." Her unfaithfulness devastated him, but it didn't destroy the love he had for her.

Have you ever been betrayed by a spouse or a friend? If so, have you forgiven that person and moved toward some type of reconciliation?

A Buyer's Benevolence

Amazingly, God's reaction to His people is the same. In spite of our adulterous ways—the fact that we've let so many other "lovers" capture the attention of our hearts—He's still committed to loving us. His reassurance of this is captured in the remarkable reconciliation of Hosea and his wandering wife recorded in Hosea 3: "The LORD said to me, 'Go, show your love to your wife again, though she is loved by another and is an adulteress. Love her as the LORD loves the Israelites, though they turn to other gods and love the sacred raisin cakes.' So I bought her" (vv. 1–2).

Hosea stood in the middle of the town square, in front of all his friends and associates, and bid for his wife, Gomer. Gomer, who'd sold herself as a prostitute. Who'd slept with whoever would have her. Who'd finally had to offer herself as a slave when men wouldn't pay for her body anymore. She probably stood on the auction block stark naked, so prospective buyers could examine the "merchandise." My guess is that after examining her, most of the men declared that she wasn't worth much. She was a tired, worn-out, used-up, old prostitute. She'd most likely been physically intimate with half the men there. I'm sure the crowd had lots of lewd remarks when the auctioneer asked if anyone was interested in buying her.

But I wonder if they got quiet when Hosea called out his bid. They all knew he was still her husband. Not only that, he was the town "preacher." Yet here he was, in the middle of the most humiliating of circumstances, buying the woman he loved. I picture him walking toward Gomer—he was the only bidder as far as we know—and reaching up to help her off the auction block. Then wrapping his coat around her nude, scarred body. Then gently leading her through the stunned crowd back toward home.

I wonder what Gomer was feeling. I wonder if she was simply numb, not fully comprehending Hosea's compassion. I wonder what she felt a few days, or weeks, or months after being bought and led away from the slave market by her own husband. By the only man who ever really loved her. Did she say "Thank you!" to Hosea a hundred times a day? Did she cook all his favorite meals and rub his tired prophet feet when he got home from work? Do you think she ever realized the enormity of his forgiveness in light of her unfaithfulness?

The Bible doesn't tell the rest of their story, but I sure hope it ended "happily ever after." The Bible does, however, tell us a few more interesting facts about Hosea. Unlike his children's names, his name has a wonderful meaning. *Hosea* means "salvation" in Hebrew; this word is very close to the word and meaning of the name *Yeshua*, or Jesus. In addition, the price Hosea paid to purchase Gomer at the slave sale was the same amount the chief priests paid Judas to betray Jesus. Isn't it amazing? God literally wrote the true story of Hosea and Gomer as an illustration of His love for those ancient, adulterous Israelites—and as a foreshadowing of the Gospel!

If you or I had written this tale, we probably wouldn't have chosen Gomer, a prostitute, to represent us as God's people. We probably would've picked a less colorful character. Certainly a woman with a better reputation! But God consistently uses very flawed people to prove His great faithfulness.

He used another prostitute, Rahab, to help God's people defeat their enemies when they first entered the Promised Land. Today Rahab's name appears in the "Hall of Faith" chapter (Hebrews 11), right alongside some of the other "spiritual giants" of Scripture. The author of Hebrews actually lauds a prostitute's faith right up there with the faith of great patriarchs such as Abraham and Moses! The apostle Matthew spotlights Rahab in his Gospel, too. As the great-great-great grandmother of King David, she is one of only five women mentioned in the genealogy of Jesus (Matthew 1).

Can you imagine? A prostitute in the direct lineage of the King of Kings and Lord of Lords!

Rahab and Gomer must've been astounded by God's compassion in light of their rebellious lifestyle. They experienced firsthand the words He spoke through Hosea: "My heart is changed within me; all my compassion is aroused.... I will heal their waywardness and love them freely, for my anger had turned away from them" (Hosea 11:8, 14:4). Like the lady of the evening who poured perfume on Christ's feet, Rahab and Gomer realized that it took a miracle of mercy to redeem them. It took a relentless kind of love that could only come from the heart of God.

I got to spend some sweet time with a former prostitute recently who reminded me of those Old Testament stories. "Peggy" spent most of her youth peddling her body on some scary streets in Nashville. She's middle-aged now, but instead of looking haggard, her face looks like that of a young woman. She literally radiates joy. Her eyes sparkle when she talks, and her speech is sprinkled with words like *rescued* and *miracles*. She laughs easily. And she can't stop talking about Jesus. I was almost jealous of her obvious joy. She seems to comprehend God's grace in a way that I haven't wrapped my mind and heart around yet. I think she's still amazed that God loves her in spite of her résumé. I found myself wanting to be more like her.

Like the movie *Pretty Woman*, Hosea's story seems like an unrealistic romance. But unlike Richard and Julia, Hosea and Gomer were real people. Their story is true. God wrote the script in order to remind us, His people, of His relentless love and amazing mercy. God loves wayward, flawed, failed, scarred people. People like Gomer. People like you and me.

15

Focusing on His Faithfulness

1. Although you may not relate to Gomer's literal prostitution, God uses the allegory of prostitution several places in Scripture (for example, Jeremiah 3 and Ezekiel 16) to illustrate how His people have been unfaithful to Him. What other "lover's" affections have you been guilty of chasing after instead of God's love?

_____

_____

_____

_____

_____

_____

2. What aspects of Gomer's story do you identify with the most? Why?

_____

_____

_____

_____

_____

_____

3. Would you characterize God's love toward you as "relentless"? If so, explain.

_____

_____

_____

_____

_____

_____

4. In what specific ways have you experienced God's relentless, pursuing love?

_____

_____

_____

_____

_____

_____

_____

_____

5. Write down your experience of being "bought" by God in spite of your wandering ways.

_____

_____

_____

_____

_____

_____

_____

_____

_____

_____

_____

_____

_____

Our lives are neither the product of blind fate nor the result of capricious chance. Every detail of them was ordained from all eternity and is now ordered by the living, reigning God. Not a hair of our heads can be touched without His permission.

—Arthur Pink

STRUGGLING WITH
SOVEREIGNTY

Every Mother's Day for as long as I can remember, a ministry in Nashville has sponsored an old-fashioned "hymn sing" at the Belle Meade Plantation, an authentic Southern plantation that's been restored and opened to the public (think *Gone with the Wind*, and you'll get the picture). It's a wonderful event that starts with a barbecue late in the afternoon, followed by the hymn sing under a big white tent on the grounds. Hundreds of people sprawl around in lawn chairs and on picnic blankets enjoying the music, while kids play tag and chase fireflies. It's a night when Nashville feels more like the fictional town of Mayberry than the metropolitan city it has become. You almost expect Aunt Bea to come around the corner in her apron and offer you a piece of hot apple pie!

I live in a cottage just a few blocks from the Belle Meade Plantation, so I walked over to the hymn sing with a few good friends and a comfortable folding chair this year. It was a beautiful summer night—just the right temperature, great music, and no mosquitoes. I was feeling nostalgic and thoroughly enjoying myself when reality bumped up against my heart. I was standing at the drink table, waiting for another glass of sweet tea and talking to a friend I hadn't seen in a long time. As we were chattily catching up with each other, a young girl (a volunteer for the organization that sponsors the event) approached us with a basket of daisies. She handed a flower to my friend—who was holding her eighteen-month-old, chocolate-chip-cookie-covered daughter—and sweetly said, "Happy Mother's Day!" Then she turned to me with a daisy in her hand and asked, "Are you a mother?"

"No," I quickly responded.

Mothers in Mourning

What I *felt* like saying was, "No, I'm not a mother, and you have no idea how much I long to be! I didn't even go to church this morning because Mother's Day gets more painful every year, and I didn't want to cry in front of my friends—who are all mothers—and ruin their special day." But I didn't want to traumatize a ten-year-old either, so I didn't say anything, I just smiled politely and watched her walk away. That innocent question from the lips of a little girl—"Are you a mother?"—reminded me of the proverb that says, "Hope deferred makes the heart sick" (Proverbs 13:12). I can't tell you how many times I've asked the question "Why should I keep on hoping when it hurts this much?" Sometimes the disappointment of unrealized hopes causes me to doubt God's sovereignty.

My best friend from high school knows all too well about hope and heart-wrenching disappointment when it comes to children. If you had known her when we were younger, you never would have imagined that Gail would struggle with anything more difficult in life than deciding which sorority to pledge in college. She was a bubbly, bouncy cheerleader who loved Jesus, her family, and just about everyone else. She was—and is—beautiful, generous, and talented. And even if you were tempted to hate her because of all that, you couldn't help but love her!

Gail married a handsome, godly guy from California named Paul Garrett a few years after college graduation. (I still have the blue velvet dress with what felt like a stainless steel bodice that I wore as her maid of honor. Despite the promises of well-intentioned brides-to-be, I have yet to rewear a bridesmaid dress after a wedding!) Anyway, Gail and Paul settled into married life in a house on a lake. He became a successful real-estate developer; she got her master's degree in counseling and began working with teenage girls in crisis.

I can't tell you how many times I've asked the question "Why should I keep on hoping when it hurts this much?" Sometimes the disappointment of

UNREALIZED HOPES

causes me to doubt God's sovereignty.

Many of the girls Gail counseled were pregnant. But Gail couldn't seem to get pregnant herself. She and Paul struggled with infertility for a long time, going to doctors, even submitting to surgery; but they still weren't able to conceive a child. Finally, after years of prayer, they felt God's unmistakable call to adopt. They decided they wanted to adopt special children who really needed them, so they listed a biracial baby as their preference.

They named their first child Philip, after Gail's dad and brother. He's a bright, adventurous little boy who keeps them on their toes. And he's blessed every corner of their lives! So when Philip was about two, they decided it was time to adopt another baby.

The second adoption went smoothly. The baby had not yet

been born, but a sonogram indicated that she was a girl. This news delighted Philip, since he had already started talking about having a sister named Caroline. Imagine the family's surprise, then, when they found out the sonogram had missed a significant detail—and their new baby turned out to be another little boy! "Caroline" sounded a bit feminine under the circumstances, so Gail and Paul chose to name him Luke instead.

Whereas Philip had been a very active infant, Luke was easy-going and compliant. Gail says she loved giving him baths each night after putting his big brother to bed, because the time alone with him was so sweet. But the sweetness turned to anguish four months later when she and Paul found out they had to give Luke back to his birth mother. Their only solace was in finding out that his paternal grandmother was a godly, compassionate woman who was committed to raising her grandson. Gail began to pray for the grandmother—and for the strength to keep going.

She said the most difficult part of the whole ordeal was that because of legal complications, she and Paul kept Luke for two and a half months after finding out they had to give him up. For ten weeks they fed him, cuddled him, changed his diapers, and rocked him to sleep at night. They watched him learn to laugh and master the art of rolling over. All the while knowing that the end was drawing near. She said it was like a slow, agonizing death. Finally, on a pretty spring day six months after bringing Luke home from the hospital, Gail and Paul drove across town to a run-down apartment and handed their baby back to his birth mother. The following excerpts are from her journal:

Monday, April 17, 2000
Luke went back to his family today. Lord, if I didn't know

that I had heard You and knew You wanted us to let go of him, I would've doubted You to the core. Please help me to adjust to this void in my life. Help me to cling to You and not escape the pain and the loss. Help me to overcome. I do believe he will be loved and cared for and that You will be with him.

Friday, April 21, 2000

Lord, You are with me. I feel like there is so much grace surrounding me right now. I feel more peaceful than I have in a long time. Thank You for pouring it out so abundantly. I pray for Luke and his family. I pray there is much rejoicing and appreciation for him. May he bless their lives and may they treat him with overwhelming kindness. May Paul, Philip, and I stay close to You. Please help us all to grieve this loss and not stuff it or displace it. Lord, I can't believe I can say "Thank You."

Monday, April 24, 2000

Well, Lord, it's finally hitting me how much I miss Luke. I don't like feeling this pain—it hurts so badly. I just want to hold him again and know that he's happy. But I may never know this, so I must trust You and Your love for Luke. Why did this have to happen, Lord? Why do I have to feel this pain? Why did I have to love him, embrace him as my own, and then lose him? Even Abraham didn't have to do this. What is the purpose?

Gail's struggle reminds me of another woman's story in the Old Testament Book of 1 Samuel:

There was a certain man from Ramathaim, a Zuphite from the hill country of Ephraim, whose name was Elkanah son of Jeroham, the son of Elihu, the son of Tohu, the son of Zuph, an Ephraimite. He had two wives; one was called Hannah and the other Peninnah. Peninnah had children, but Hannah had none.

Year after year this man went up from his town to worship and sacrifice to the LORD Almighty at Shiloh, were Hophni and Phinehas, the two sons of Eli, were priests of the LORD.

Whenever the day came for Elkanah to sacrifice, he would give portions of the meat to his wife Peninnah and to all her sons and daughters. But to Hannah he gave a double portion because he loved her, and the LORD had closed her womb. And because the LORD had closed her womb, her rival kept provoking her in order to irritate her. This went on year after year. (vv. 1–7)

If you can get past the genealogy and all the strange sounding words, this is some story! The brokenhearted heroine is a woman named Hannah who also struggled with infertility. Her husband adored her anyway, but his other wife (polygamy was the cultural norm during this period of history), named Peninnah, persecuted and ridiculed her. Finally Hannah went on a starvation diet because she wanted children so badly, and she'd had about all she could take of Peninnah's pestering. Escaping into a temple to cry and pray, Hannah no doubt asked some of the same questions Gail did when she was alone:

"Why does this have to happen, Lord?"

"Why do I have to feel this pain?"

"What is the purpose?"

Have you ever asked one of those questions? Have you ever been so overcome with pain and disappointment that you doubted God's sovereignty?

Finite Minds, Fickle Faith

If the answer is "yes," you're not alone. Those questions about God's purpose in pain strike a familiar note in the chord of human history. The doubt and disbelief caused by loss and longing permeate every denominational, economic, cultural, and historical segment of society. And God is certainly not surprised by our suspicion. He formed us—fickle faith and all—and knows that at some time or another, we will all wonder about the absolute sovereignty of our Creator.

C. S. Lewis penned weighty words laced with questions and uncertainty after the death of his wife, Joy Davidson. She was the love of his life, but an unexpected one. After spending his youth and most of his middle age as a bachelor (some say a cantankerous chauvinist!), he married Joy in 1956. He was almost sixty; she was forty-two.

In the beginning, their marriage was more of a benevolent gesture on Lewis's part. Prior to their nuptials, Joy was just a good friend. She was also deathly ill with cancer and not expected to live. So C. S. Lewis took her hand in marriage and gave her and her two little boys a home. Soon after the wedding, however, Joy's cancer miraculously went into remission, and a very real romance grew strong and deep between them. During that brief, sweet season, Lewis wrote, "I never expected to have, in my sixties, the happiness that passed me by in my twenties."

> *God is certainly not surprised by our suspicion. He formed us—*
> **FICKLE FAITH**
> *and all—and knows that at some time or another, we will all wonder about the absolute sovereignty of our Creator.*

Sadly, Joy's cancer returned with a vengeance in the fall of 1959, after just three years of marriage. She died the next summer. Two of the last things she said to her husband before she died were "You have made me happy" and "I am at peace with God." Those close to the couple said her death devastated Lewis, and he never fully recovered. The following excerpt comes from *A Grief Observed,* the painfully honest journal he wrote after Joy died:

> Am I, for instance, just sidling back to God because I know that if there's any road to H. [the pet name he calls Joy in his journal], it runs through Him? But then of course I know perfectly well that He can't be used as a road. If you're approaching Him not as the goal but as a road, not as an end but as a means, you're not really approaching Him at all….
>
> Lord, are these your real terms: Can I meet H. again only if I learn to love you so much that I don't care whether I meet her or not? Consider, Lord, how it looks to us. What would anyone think of me if I said to the boys, "No toffee now. But when you've grown up and don't really want toffee, you shall have as much of it as you choose"?
>
> If I knew that to be eternally divided from H. and eternally forgotten by her would add a greater joy and splendor to her being, of course I'd say "Fire ahead." Just as if, on earth, I could have cured her cancer by never seeing her again, I'd have arranged never to see her again. I'd have had to. Any decent person would. But that's quite different. That's not the situation I'm in.
>
> When I lay those questions before God I get no answer. But a rather special sort of "no answer." It is not the locked door. It is more like a silent, certainly not uncompassionate, gaze. As though He shook His head not in refusal but waiving the question. Like, "Peace, child; you don't understand."[1]

These words by C. S. Lewis remind us that *trusting* in God's sovereignty doesn't mean we have to *understand* it. I certainly don't *understand* why trials and tragedies happen to His beloved children. But neither do I think that every seemingly cruel circumstance is divinely causative—that God *causes* it to happen. And while I firmly believe that our omnipotent God never initiates anything inherently evil or sinful, I certainly can't explain why He allows horrible things to take place. Simplistic answers trivialize suffering, and anything else is speculative. The bottom line is that our minds are far too finite to understand the perfect wisdom God uses to govern our world.

Blind Trust and Two Babies

Although I'm still daft enough to try to dissect God's sovereignty at times, I have learned that there is usually profound providence in pain. Because it has been in my own grief that God has revealed depths of grace I didn't know before. Faltering steps of sorrow have taken me closer to the heart of God. My desperation for His comforting presence has been the close companion of deep sadness.

And frankly, I think mature trust in God's sovereignty requires a certain release of human understanding. His exact purpose in pain may never be completely clear in our natural life. But the resulting blindness is a rich fertilizer for our faith. Gail told me that "blind trust" was one of the biggest lessons she learned in giving up Luke. We were talking about the tension between trusting God and not understanding His providence in suffering when she said, "I don't even want to be in control anymore. I'd rather know He's in control, even if I'm not sure what the future holds. Even if it's painful."

The end of Hannah's story in 1 Samuel illustrates what Gail and I were talking about. After years of longing and after begging God for a baby in the temple, Hannah got pregnant. Nine months later she gave birth to a little boy named Samuel. And then, in an act of supreme trust in God's sovereignty, Hannah gave her baby back to the Giver of Life:

> After he was weaned, she took the boy with her, young as he was, along with a three-year-old bull, an ephah of flour and a

skin of wine, and brought him to the house of the LORD at Shiloh. When they had slaughtered the bull, they brought the boy to Eli, and she said to him, "As surely as you live, my lord, I am the woman who stood here beside you praying to the LORD. I prayed for this child, and the LORD has granted me what I asked of him. So now I give him to the LORD. For his whole life he will be given over to the LORD." And he worshiped the LORD there. (1 Samuel 1:24–28)

After Hannah handed baby Samuel over to Eli to be raised as the next leader of Israel, she did a remarkable thing: She rejoiced in God's goodness. Her phenomenal prayer is recorded in 1 Samuel 2:1–10: "My heart rejoices in the Lord…. There is no one holy like the LORD; there is no one besides you; there is no Rock like our God…. For the foundations of the earth are the LORD's; upon them he has set the world…."

Have you ever had to let go of a loved one? Can you imagine rejoicing in the "letting go"?

Hannah and Gail and C. S. Lewis learned to trust and rejoice in God's sovereignty, even when they didn't understand it. The suffering that accompanied their love and loss was made bearable by believing in—not necessarily understanding—God's absolute authority over all things. They walked headlong into intense grief and found out that God really is faithful. His love really is relentless and abiding. He didn't leave them alone! In the midst of sorrow, they found healing in His presence. And thus, in their pain, they found profound peace.

Even unexpected gifts. God blessed Hannah with five more children, three boys and two girls. And my dear friend Gail got to buy pink booties after all.

Caroline Ruth Garrett was born on December 5, 2000. She is the baby sister of one very proud four-year-old boy who named her years before she finally came home.

Focusing on His Faithfulness

1. Describe a recent time of uncertainty or grief when you felt like you received a silent "no answer" from God.

_____

_____

_____

_____

_____

_____

_____

_____

2. Did God's relative silence when you were in pain cause you to doubt His sovereignty? How can you now see Him at work in that difficult time?

_____

_____

_____

_____

_____

_____

_____

_____

3. Compare Hannah's prayer in 1 Samuel 2:1–10 with Mary's song (the Magnificat) in Luke 1:46–55. Why do you think these women were able to rejoice, in light of their circumstances?

_____

_____

_____

_____

_____

_____

_____

_____

4. Do you agree with the statement "Suffering that accompanies love and loss is made bearable by believing in—not necessarily understanding—God's absolute authority over all things"? Why or why not?

_____

_____

_____

_____

_____

_____

_____

_____

5. Write a prayer about the most difficult or disappointing situation in your life right now. When you finish writing, compare what you've written to the words of Hannah and Mary.

_____

_____

_____

_____

_____

_____

_____

_____

_____

_____

_____

_____

It is an unspeakable mercy that the Father comes with His chastisement, makes the world round us all dark and unattractive, leads us to feel more deeply our sinfulness, and for a time lose our joy in what was becoming so dangerous. He does it in the hope that, when we have found our rest in Christ in time of trouble, we shall learn to choose abiding in Him as our only portion; and when the affliction is removed, have so grown more firmly into Him, that in prosperity He still shall be our only joy.

—Andrew Murray

THE NECESSITY OF
NEEDINESS

One of my friends is a pretty and outgoing southern blonde named Eva. She's married to a wonderful man-who-should-be-cloned-for-single-women-everywhere named Andrew, and they have two little girls, Abigail and Audrey. Eva's a great cook, a great Bible teacher, a great tennis player, and a great friend. She also happens to be a paraplegic.

We met a few years after Eva was in a car accident that left her paralyzed from the waist down, so I've always known her in a wheelchair. I'm used to folding it up and sticking it in the trunk, looking for ramps when we go to the mall, and making sure doorways are wide enough for her to roll through. I don't gasp anymore when she does wheelies to clear the curb or when she presses the remote to activate the nifty robotic gadget that grabs and whips the wheelchair into the storage compartment on the car roof. (Although I did gasp when the robotic gadget whacked her in the forehead one day when she leaned out of the car too far to say hi!) I don't really even notice her wheelchair anymore. It's just a normal part of our entourage—kind of like my purse, which is almost as heavy!

However, I'm continually surprised by the way some people treat Eva when we're in public. Several times waiters have turned to me and said, "And what will your friend be having?" as if the food-choice area of her frontal lobe was paralyzed, too. Salesclerks have asked me questions about the clothes she was trying on, as if her fashion sense was flung out the window in the accident. Others talk to her very slowly and very loudly, enunciating every syllable with care and concentration—obviously thinking that because her legs don't work, her hearing is shot, as well.

I get just a little grouchy with these ignoramuses and their myopic view of a woman who towers over most people in faith, integrity, and humor. But the people who inflame me to the highest echelons of grouchiness have been condescending Christians—people who say Eva wouldn't need a wheelchair if she had more faith.

Eva called me a few months ago to tell me yet another story about someone like that. She said a woman at a retreat (where Eva was the keynote speaker) was insistent about praying for her. The woman was emphatic about her ability to "heal" Eva's paralysis and more or less demanded that Eva let her lay hands on her and pray. She thanked the woman for her zeal and patiently explained that thousands of people had prayed for her *physical* healing for twenty years, to no avail. She further explained that although she knew God could heal her body in a flash if He chose to, He had matured her to a place of rest and peace with her paralysis. Eva told Polly Persistence that she believed God was using her "handicap" for His glory and that she firmly believed He was sovereign regardless of her physical condition. Then she graciously told the woman that if she still wanted to pray for her healing, she would appreciate a prayer for the healing of her impatience so that she could be a better wife and mother.

Well, talk about throwing gas on a fire! Eva's response made that woman really mad. She pursed her lips, set her face in a haughty expression, and looked down at Eva sitting in her wheelchair. Then she said with patronizing pity, "Don't you want to get up out of that chair and walk?" Ugh! After Eva told me the story, I wanted to call that woman and give her a lecture about compassion. I was so irritated! I couldn't believe that another woman—at a Christian retreat, no less—could be so self-righteous and smug.

The people who inflame me to the highest echelons of grouchiness have been CONDESCENDING CHRISTIANS— people who say Eva wouldn't need a wheelchair if she had more faith.

Have you ever met someone like that—a smug, self-righteous Christian? Do you think anyone has ever described you that way?

That woman has no idea what it's like to be on the porch in a wheelchair when your six-year-old gets off the school bus crying, and you have to wait for her to walk up the steps before you can hug her and ask "What's wrong, sweetie?" She doesn't know what it feels like to roll down the aisle and wish you could stand up face to face with your new husband when the preacher says, "You may now kiss your bride." And she doesn't know the anguish of hearing your baby cry out in the night, knowing that it will take several minutes to transfer from the bed to the wheelchair and roll down the hall to her crib to make sure she's okay. Yet she had the audacity to ask "Don't you want to get up out of that chair and walk?"

Immanuel's Inquiry

How callous, how cruel, to question a woman who's never been able to stand up and kiss her husband or go for a walk with her little girls about her desire to get out of her wheelchair! Yet that's almost exactly the same question Jesus asked the paralytic who was lying by the pool of Bethesda in John 5:

> Some time later, Jesus went up to Jerusalem for a feast of the Jews. Now there is in Jerusalem near the Sheep Gate a pool, which in Aramaic is called Bethesda and which is surrounded by five covered colonnades. Here a great number of disabled people used to lie—the blind, the lame, the paralyzed. One who was there had been an invalid for thirty-eight years. When Jesus saw him lying there and learned that he had been in this condition for a long time, he asked him, "Do you want to get well?"
> "Sir," the invalid replied, "I have no one to help me into the pool when the water is stirred. While I am trying to get in, someone else goes down ahead of me." (vv. 1–7)

The Jews believed miracles happened at the Pool of Bethesda when there was a ripple in the water. They thought the ripples were caused by the very hand of God. So when the water stirred, the sick scrambled to get in as fast as they could, believing they would be healed of their infirmities. But this poor man couldn't even drag his crippled body to the water in time to get wet when it counted. He'd been at the pool for years, probably dependent on the mercy of friends or neighbors to drop him off and pick him up. Or maybe he lived there, hoping for handouts from those coming and going to the Temple, which was just a stone's throw away. We don't know his whole story, but we do know that no one cared enough to sit with him and help carry him to the water. Can you imagine how frustrating it was for him—month after month and year after year—watching others cut in front of him and shout "Hallelujahs" when they stepped out of the pool healed?

Most of us are still foolish when it comes to neediness. We typically DISGUISE OUR OWN and have disdain for everyone else's.

At first glance Jesus' question, "Do you want to get well?" sounds almost as rude as the question the woman asked Eva. Yet all throughout the Gospels, Jesus confronted people with that type of question. He compelled men and women to acknowledge their "sickness" and their desire to get well with words or with actions.

That's what He did with the rich young ruler in Matthew 19. Jesus made him face the reality that his possessions couldn't heal the discontent caused by his spiritual hunger. But this adolescent heir's death grip on his trinkets made it impossible for him to reach out to the Great Physician. The young man went away sad—and sick at heart. And remember the woman at the well in John 4? Her story had a much better ending because she admitted that she was needy. When she recognized that the men in her life had never quenched her thirst for affection, Jesus gave her Living Water to satisfy her parched soul.

One went away sad; the other left rejoicing and even organized her town's first revival! Their stories underscore the fact that our world is full of physical and emotional pain, and we can't heal ourselves. Yet most of us are still foolish when it comes to neediness. We typically disguise our own and have disdain for everyone else's.

In fact, I think one of the most tragic flaws in Christendom today is our reluctance to admit we're sick and need divine help.

Inexcusable or Inevitable?

My friends will tell you that I'm a terrible patient. I really don't like admitting that I'm sick. I take after my mother, who is a wonderful woman but a proud stoic when it comes to physical pain. I can't remember her ever going to the doctor when we were growing up. And she wouldn't set foot in a hospital unless she had a compound fracture and couldn't poke the bone back in herself! She's a cute, petite, well-mannered, and well-dressed woman—but her pain threshold is more like that of a burly, ax-swinging, beer-chugging lumberjack. (My apologies to all small-boned, teetotaling woodworkers—I know you're out there.) Therefore, the subtle message in our home was that if it wasn't pneumonia or a compound fracture, you were going to be just fine!

Until recently I thought my ability to handle pain without being a "sissy" was an admirable character trait. I was proud of the fact that I played college volleyball with a broken ankle, fractured wrist, and various other sprains and strains. My masochistic mindset didn't mature with middle age, either. I continued to drag my aching, over-thirty body up and down mountains on skis, bikes, or snowboards, even after spectacular, bloody-knees spills. And I rarely stayed home from work when I was sick, oblivious to the dirty looks from coworkers, friends, and loved ones concerned about contagious germs.

But then, a few years ago, I learned how silly and dangerous it was to grit my teeth when faced with real pain or serious sickness. I was trail-running with a friend on Pike's Peak, and we had to race six miles down the mountain to escape a spring thunder-storm. When I jumped in my car to drive home, my back was hurting so badly that I winced every time I hit a bump in the road. My eyes watered whenever I shifted in my seat. But I thought, *Oh, it's probably just a bad pulled muscle or something.* Besides, I've had lower back pain ever since I was run over by a car at the age of eleven (that's a whole other story), so I decided that the pounding from our downhill dash had just aggravated my normal backache. I took a shower, gobbled some ibuprofen, and raced to the airport for a business trip. By the time I got back to Colorado a few days later, I could barely walk. So I bit the bullet and went to a doctor.

If you've ever been to the doctor for something more serious than a cold, you've probably experienced the *physician's pain quiz.* That's when he or she asks you to rate your pain on a level from one to ten, with one being for slight pain and ten representing pass-out pain. I don't like that question. How in the world do you assign a number value to your pain level? Besides, I don't want to sound like some hysterical hypochondriac; so as long as I'm conscious, I figure it's less than five.

That explains why, when the doctor asked me to number my back pain that day, I gave it a three or four. He poked around a little and then told me that the problem was probably just a pulled muscle. He said I should continue taking ibuprofen and suggested that I rent some good movies and "lay low" for the weekend.

Of course, my back hurt worse than ever after a few weeks, so I listened to the advice of my "normal" friends—the ones who don't think it's admirable to pull out stitches with tweezers at home rather than going to the doctor's office and having a professional do it—

and made an appointment with a back specialist. I think I told him my back pain was now about a four and a half. He poked and prodded a little more, took an X-ray, and then confirmed the original diagnosis of a pulled muscle. I shuffled out of the office embarrassed that my once robust pain threshold was shriveling to that of Minnie Mouse. I decided I would never bother these brilliant, busy doctors again unless I was sure that death was imminent. And I decided to ignore their advice to rest, because surely the cure for my wimpy back was to get in better shape. So I ran, biked, and hiked harder—and gobbled down extra-strength ibuprofen.

A few months later, I went on a mountain-biking-mama trip to Moab, Utah, with some girls from Vail who are ski instructors and fitness specialists. For several days I scrambled over boulders and breathlessly biked up sandstone cliffs, trying to keep up with them. My back was on fire, and pain was shooting up and down my legs; but I wasn't about to complain, because I didn't want to look like a baby in the presence of the bionic bombshells. However, when I crawled out of the tent on the last day of our "vacation," I was a little worried that my right leg was dragging behind my left and I couldn't feel my toes.

I sheepishly called the doctor again, and he sent me to have an MRI test. He called back with the results a few days later, apologizing profusely for having misdiagnosed two completely ruptured discs. He said he never would've guessed that I had such a severe back injury because my complaints about pain were so minor. I was then transferred on emergency basis to a renowned surgeon who works with some of the athletes at the Olympic Training Center. Evidently my doctor told him I was a stubborn, athletic has-been.

After sternly reprimanding me for reckless behavior, the neurosurgeon said mine was the worse case of lumbar disc rupture he'd seen in a long time. The nerve damage was irreparable, my right leg had atrophied an inch, and I was dangerously close to losing control of my bladder functions. He scheduled the operation for the following morning. (I did ask if he'd consider postponing surgery until my bottom atrophied a few inches, too!)

The surgery was relatively successful, given the state of my battered lower back. But I can't run anymore, and I had to give up my dreams of becoming an international limbo star. There's a really cute pair of kickboxing shoes gathering dust in my closet because the class almost put me in traction. Simply rolling out of bed, stepping into pants, and putting on socks have become grimacing gyrations that can only be described as "Twister torture." And I'm facing another surgery to fuse my lumber vertebrae together. I really wish I had told the doctor in the beginning that my pain level was at least an eleven! Pretending it didn't hurt, that I could handle the pain by myself, was foolish.

Neediness is a **SPIRITUAL NECESSITY.** *The whole point of the Gospel is that we can't save ourselves!*

How about you? Are you as stubborn as I am when it comes to asking for help when you're sick or hurting?

One of the biggest mental mistakes I've made has been thinking that sickness or weakness is inexcusable rather than inevitable. And that truth applies to our souls even more so than our bodies. Neediness is a spiritual necessity. The whole point of the Gospel is that we can't save ourselves! And Scripture is replete with examples of strong spiritual leaders who personify neediness:

- Moses had a speech impediment and didn't think he could handle the job of leading the Israelites. He actually asked God to send someone else. (Exodus 4:10–13)
- Gideon—whom God affectionately called "mighty warrior" in Judges 6:12—hid from his enemies in a winepress because he was mighty wimpy!
- In their boat during a storm, the frightened disciples needed Jesus to calm their anxious hearts along with some very high seas. (Mark 4:35–41)

Immanuel's Invitation

The good news highlighted by these biblical characters is that God is familiar with our neediness! Unlike the woman who was rude to Eva or the doctor who recommended movies when I needed major surgery, He knows exactly what we need. The Bible says that Jesus is a "man of sorrows," more than acquainted with every grief we bear (Isaiah 53:3). He is not an aloof bystander dispassionately observing us while we grin and bear it. He was literally broken for us—so that our pain wouldn't have to be permanent. First Peter 2:24 says, "He himself bore our sins in his body on the tree, so that we might die to sins and live for righteousness; by his wounds you have been healed."

The question Jesus posed to the man at the Pool of Bethesda, "Do you want to get well?" wasn't callous or cruel. It was a compassionate invitation to be healed. His inquiry was laced with love. The moment the man told Jesus that he couldn't crawl to the pool fast enough when Jehovah turned on the Jacuzzi—thereby acknowledging his pain and his inability to heal himself—Jesus said, "Get up! Pick up your mat and walk" (John 5:8).

Jesus compels us to acknowledge our weakness so that we can be strengthened, to recognize our sickness so that He can make us well. Our neediness really is necessary:

> While Jesus was having dinner at Matthew's house, many tax collectors and "sinners" came and ate with him and his disciples. When the Pharisees saw this, they asked his disciples, "Why does your teacher eat with tax collectors and 'sinners'?"
> On hearing this, Jesus said, "It is not the healthy who need a doctor, but the sick. But go and learn what this means: 'I desire mercy, not sacrifice.' For I have not come to call the righteous, but sinners." (Matthew 9:10–13)

I've learned a lot from my friend Eva. The world we live in may look at her wheelchair and call her handicapped—but I don't. Not anymore. Eva can't walk, but her love for Jesus runs rampant. Her legs have atrophied, but her heart for Him is amazingly healthy. A car accident caused her broken back, but it also caused her to be more dependent on God's faithfulness. In her chair she experiences His affectionate intimacy and relentless love in a way few people ever do. And the results are absolutely beautiful.

Focusing on His Faithfulness

1. Do you tend to be more of a "sissy" or a "stoic" when it comes to physical pain? Give an example.

_____

_____

_____

_____

_____

2. Do you usually ask for help or turn into a hermit when you're hurt? Why?

_____

_____

_____

_____

_____

_____

_____

3. What's the level of heart pain you've been experiencing lately? What's causing it?

_____

_____

_____

_____

_____

_____

_____

4. Who's the most beautiful "broken" person you know? What's the key to his or her beauty?

_____

_____

_____

_____

_____

_____

5. Write down some of the areas in your life in which you really need help from the Great Physician.

_____

_____

_____

_____

_____

_____

_____

_____

_____

We are buoyed by a confident trust in the character of God. Even when all we see are the tangled threads on the backside of life's tapestry, we know that God is good and is out to do us good always.

—Richard Foster

PROBLEMS WITH
PERCEPTION

I used to love hiking and running when I lived in Colorado. After a hard day at work, there was nothing more relaxing and restorative to me than getting away from ringing phones and urgent e-mails to the tranquil beauty of the mountains. When I didn't have time to drive to a remote wilderness area, I would do the next best thing and go to some of the great parks in town. One, called Pulpit Rock Park, was just a few miles from my condo, and I went there a lot during the week.

But then reports of criminal activity at Pulpit Rock Park started circulating in the news. Grim-faced television reporters gave details about several rapes that had occurred within the park and said police were also looking for a man who'd exposed himself to some unsuspecting park users. TV and newspapers specifically warned women about running or hiking alone on park trails until the rapist and/or flasher was apprehended.

Despite the publicized concern, I went to the park alone one incredible fall evening. I inhaled the crisp mountain air deeply and started jogging up one of the trails, ignoring the warning signs posted on trees as I ran by. I just couldn't imagine a criminal lurking in the park on such a glorious day!

For a few miles I ran in perfect solitude through majestic evergreens on the twisting mountain path. Then I came to a high alpine meadow. But just as I was about to break from the trees into the clearing, I stopped dead in my tracks. Panting with visible, white-frosty breaths, I tried to keep from panicking at the sight directly in front of me: A naked man was sitting on a picnic bench about fifty feet away, his hands between his legs. I couldn't believe it! Here I was enjoying a nice jog through the park, and I'd run right into this loser's lair!

I knew he was going to notice me any second, and I had to act fast. But I didn't want to risk turning around and racing back through the woods for several miles with him in hot pursuit. This naked nerd was probably the flasher, I figured, and I suddenly remembered reading somewhere that men who expose themselves for thrills are typically cowards and nonconfrontive. So I quickly decided to be the aggressor and catch him off guard before he could do something trashy. I took a big breath, jumped out of the woods, and ran straight toward him, screaming "Hey!" in a deep, menacing tone and waving my arms over my head. I'd read somewhere else that talking in a loud, low voice and waving your arms would scare away most wild animals. And it worked, because the man jumped straight up off the bench in apparent shock!

Then, clad in tiny blue running shorts—clothing I hadn't noticed from my vantage point at the edge of the woods—he ran away in the opposite direction. A little dog—whom he'd obviously been petting between his legs—scampered behind him. As he sprinted across the meadow, he nervously looked back over his shoulder at me several times. No doubt thinking, *I need to call the newspaper and tell them that the perpetrator is a loud girl in lime green shorts!* He's probably still in therapy somewhere, petrified to jog alone anymore!

I could've sworn he was naked. And from the way he was sitting—well, it sure looked like he was doing something illegal. But it was starting to get dark, and I couldn't see clearly. Plus I was a little too panicked to pay close attention. As a result, what I thought I saw wasn't reality.

It's amazing how wrong we can be—and how much damage we can cause—when our sight is impaired! Scaring innocent men loitering in mountain meadows is mild compared to some of the more serious consequences that can result from cloudy vision. People are killed every year during hunting season because some hunter squinting in the fog

Whether the cause is bad lighting or big obstacles, POOR PERCEPTION *can be very dangerous. Especially when it comes to the spiritual arena—to our view of God.*

before daybreak mistakes a John Doe for a real one. And every war ever fought has a casualty number attributed to "friendly fire"—innocent people killed because their comrades mistook them for the enemy.

Clearly, whether the cause is bad lighting or big obstacles, poor perception can be very dangerous. Especially when it comes to the spiritual arena—to our view of God.

Stubborn Men and Miraculous Mules

Most of us at some time or another have a very flawed view of God. When we can't see around the "obstacles" of circumstances, or when we have to squint in the emotional "darkness" of trials and tribulations, our skewed spiritual perspective causes us to distort God and His directions to us. Instead of waiting for His voice to lead us, we often charge ahead blindly—usually to our own demise.

How do you view obstacles and darkness in your life? Do you see them as nuisances to get over or grope through—or do you see them as a yield sign from Yahweh?

Balaam, a colorful character in the Old Testament, is probably the best example of someone who had serious spiritual sight problems and difficulty with divine directions. Numbers 22, 23, and 24 tell the whole story of this bad-boy psychic with a talking donkey:

> Then the Israelites traveled to the plains of Moab and camped along the Jordan across from Jericho. Now Balak son of Zippor saw all that Israel had done to the Amorites, and Moab was terrified because there were so many people. Indeed, Moab was filled with dread because of the Israelites. The Moabites said to the elders of Midian, "This horde is going to lick up everything around us, as an ox licks up the grass of the field." So Balak son of Zippor, who was king of Moab at that time, sent messengers to summon Balaam son of Beor, who was at Pethor, near the River, in his native land. (Numbers 22:1–5)

The reason this king with a weird name sent for Balaam was because Balaam was a "diviner." King Balak and his Mesopotamian followers believed that diviners could predict the future—and even change the course of the future. (That's the same reason millions of people in our culture pay several dollars a minute to talk to some turban-wearing "psychic" on TV.) The king wanted the Israelites stopped, so he sent for Balaam, promising him a fortune if he'd just put a curse on the Israelites and drive them away. But God spoke to Balaam in a dream and told him, "Do not go with them. You must not put a curse on those people, because they are blessed" (Numbers 22:12). So the next morning Balaam got up and told the king's messengers, "Go back to your own country, for the LORD has refused to let me go with you" (v. 13).

King Balak, however, would not take "no" for an answer. He sent a second group of more distinguished representatives to Balaam, promising an even bigger bounty if he'd put a curse on the Israelites. And after some wheeling and dealing—and another dream with directions from God—Balaam saddled his donkey and took off with the princes of Moab. But apparently Balaam hadn't paid close enough attention to God's directions in the dream. Because when Balaam didn't follow those directions correctly, God was angry—and He sent an angelic emissary to make His intentions unmistakably clear.

> But God was very angry when he went, and the angel of the LORD stood in the road to oppose him. Balaam was riding on his donkey, and his two servants were with him. When the donkey saw the angel of the LORD standing in the road with a drawn sword in his hand, she turned off the road into a field. Balaam beat her to get her back on the road.
>
> Then the angel of the LORD stood in a narrow path between two vineyards, with walls on both sides. When the donkey saw the angel of the LORD, she pressed close to the wall, crushing Balaam's foot against it. So he beat her again.
>
> Then the angel of the LORD moved on ahead and stood in a narrow place where there was no room to turn, either to the right or to the left. When the donkey saw the angel of the LORD, she lay down under Balaam, and he was angry and beat her with his staff. Then the LORD opened the donkey's mouth,

and she said to Balaam, "What have I done to you to make you beat me these three times?"

Balaam answered the donkey, "You have made a fool of me! If I had a sword in my hand, I would kill you right now."

The donkey said to Balaam, "Am I not your own donkey, which you have always ridden, to this day? Have I been in the habit of doing this to you?"

"No," he said.

Then the LORD opened Balaam's eyes, and he saw the angel of the LORD standing in the road with his sword drawn. So he bowed low and fell facedown.

The angel of the LORD asked him, "Why have you beaten your donkey these three times? I have come here to oppose you because your path is a reckless one before me. The donkey saw me and turned away from me these three times. If she had not turned away, I would certainly have killed you by now, but I would have spared her."

Balaam said to the angel of the LORD, "I have sinned. I did not realize you were standing in the road to oppose me." (Numbers 22:22–34)

Reading the Road Signs

Isn't this a great story? I think it's hilarious that Balaam had an entire conversation with this Old Testament Mr. Ed before God ever revealed that He had empowered the donkey to speak! What in the world was Balaam thinking? Donkeys aren't usually very chatty creatures. Why didn't he faint in shock when she uttered the first word? He must've been one dopey diviner!

And he definitely needed new spiritual glasses, because he completely missed clear signals from the Lord three times. Instead of pausing at the angel crossing, he was determined to plow on through, adding animal cruelty to his oblivious obstinacy. God tried to steer him away from the reckless path he was taking, but he didn't see the road signs! As a result, his clouded vision almost got him killed. If it weren't for his discussion with the tolerant donkey, he would've ended up quite dead on that narrow path.

Although I've never argued with an animal—at least not one that talked back—I've definitely missed God's cues and taken the wrong path at times. And much like Balaam, my first response to obstacles is usually to plow right through them. But God is teaching me to pause and pray before plunging ahead. I'm learning that darkness and hurdles are often heaven-sent, protecting us from our own rash responses and training us to wait for divine direction and guidance.

My first response to obstacles is usually to plow right through them. But God is teaching me to PAUSE AND PRAY *before plunging ahead.*

If you're facing a wall, pound it with prayer before swinging a sledgehammer. If you can't see clearly in the shadows of your circumstances, slow down and wait for God to illuminate the path He wants you to walk. And be patient. God might not remove the entire obstacle or reveal the end of the trail. His plan usually takes longer than ours, and His guidance is usually one step at a time.

Memory Loss and Lessons from Mom

Sadly, although God got his attention, Balaam obviously didn't listen for long. You'd think that a spiritual lesson from an animal's mouth would never be forgotten. But Jewish history tells us that after hearing a donkey, seeing an angel, and blessing the Israelites instead of cursing them, Balaam still embraced paganism and turned away from God. He forgot everything his four-legged friend said, and his eyes clouded over again with idolatry. Later, when God pronounced His judgment against the Midianites, Balaam was killed in battle, leaving only a legacy of shame. The Bible includes him in a passage about sinful and arrogant men: "They have left the straight way and wandered off to follow the way of Balaam son of Beor, who loved the wages of wickedness. But he was rebuked for his wrongdoing by a donkey—a beast without speech—who spoke with a man's voice and restrained the prophet's madness" (2 Peter 2:15–16).

Have you ever forgotten a lesson God clearly taught you? If so, how was your spiritual vision blurred by pride or fear?

About ten years ago I had forgotten some basic and powerful promises from God. I was disillusioned and depressed and called my mom from a phone booth, gulping back sobs as I told her that my life was falling apart. I was in the middle of a difficult job change, a good friend had been killed, and I'd just found out that another friend was having an affair. I said that I couldn't see any light at the end of the tunnel, and I didn't know which way to turn. Mom listened for a while and then told me that I should study the Book of Isaiah. She said that Isaiah had a lot to say about dark places and God's direction.

When we're in the dark and can't see very well, we need to **TRUST** *God. We have to take time to let our spiritual pupils dilate.*

I wasn't too excited about her suggestion. Instead of telling me to read Isaiah, I wanted her to Fed Ex a plane ticket to some place far away where she'd lovingly made me reservations at a fabulous spa. I really didn't feel like listening to the lessons of an Old Testament prophet, and I sure didn't feel like taking a long pause filled with prayer. I felt like curling up into a ball and crying with a box of dark chocolates nearby!

Thankfully, mom didn't fall prey to my pity party. Because when it comes to spiritual insight, the prophet Isaiah is just as enlightening as Balaam the diviner was dumb.

I spent several months wading through the words of Isaiah and grew to love how he uses darkness as a metaphor for those unsure times in our lives when we can't "see" through our circumstances. He obviously memorized the lessons Balaam forgot, because his book is full of wonderful instruction. One of my favorite tutoring passages comes from a section called the Servant Songs:

> Who among you fears the LORD and obeys the word of his servant? Let him who walks in the dark, who has no light, trust in the name of the LORD and rely on his God. But now, all you who light fires and provide yourselves with flaming torches, go, walk in the light of your fires and of the torches you have set ablaze. This is what you shall receive from my hand: You will lie down in torment. (Isaiah 50:10–11)

Mushrooms aren't the only things that grow in the dark; so does our faith. The message of Isaiah's metaphor is simple: When we're in the dark and can't see very well, we need to trust God. We have to take time to let our spiritual pupils dilate. If we trust in our own ability to make the darkness disappear, we're going to be really sorry. Lying down in torment isn't pleasant.

Reading Isaiah didn't make the dark clouds in my life immediately go away. It didn't make the obstacles I was facing dramatically disappear. But the words he wrote reminded me to pause and pray and look to the Lord for direction, instead of being a baby—or bull-headed like Balaam!

As we wrap up this chapter, I want to say a few words to those of you who don't identify with the mind-set of plowing over obstacles or plunging ahead when you can't see. Your personality might not be an aggressive Type A. Maybe you don't struggle with charging ahead; you struggle more with getting out of bed! Instead of the hyperactivity that I'm so quick to display, you're more hyper-hesitant. Waiting isn't difficult for you—change is. But whether we're determined to take charge or determined to stay safe, the key to walking successfully in the dark isn't in the *pausing*; it's in the *praying*. Because merely waiting without seeking God's direction is as fruitless as herding cats!

God is teaching some of us to be still and listen, and He's teaching others to hear His mandate to move. To get up and take a step of faith—even when we aren't sure of where we're walking. Because God promises to guide us every step of the way. He whispers directions along with endearments. "I will lead the blind by ways they have not known, along unfamiliar paths I will guide them," He says in Isaiah 42:16. "I will turn the darkness into light before them and make the rough places smooth. These are the things I will do; I will not forsake them."

There will be times in life when we can't see the trail. Times when we get sidetracked by a big bump in the road. But we can rest assured that in those times, God will always take us by our sweaty palms and lead us safely on. Because His compassion never fails, and His mercies are relentless. They are new every time the alarm clock goes off.

Focusing on His Faithfulness

1. What are some of the significant spiritual lessons you've forgotten in times of stress or complacency? How could remembering those lessons have made a difference?

_____

_____

_____

_____

_____

_____

_____

_____

_____

_____

2. Describe a "dark" area—a circumstance you can't see past—that's currently clouding your spiritual vision.

_____

_____

_____

_____

_____

_____

_____

_____

_____

_____

3. When life gets uncertain, do you tend to plunge ahead—or pull the covers over your head? Are you more the "take charge" or timid type? Do you think God is telling you to *walk* or to *wait* in whatever difficult circumstance you find yourself in right now?

_____

_____

_____

_____

_____

_____

_____

_____

_____

4. Read Isaiah 54 and Psalm 91. Consider memorizing key verses from each of these chapters and/or writing them on note cards that you post in prominent places (refrigerator door, car visor, etc.). Write a verse you want to memorize below.

_____

_____

_____

_____

_____

_____

_____

_____

_____

5. Describe your response to the terrorist tragedies of September 11, 2001. How have you seen God's activity in that event?

_____

_____

_____

_____

_____

_____

_____

_____

The deep truth is that our human suffering need not be an obstacle to the joy and peace we so desire, but can become, instead, the means to it.

—Henri Nouwen

FALTERING FOREFATHERS

I've had the incredible opportunity to visit Israel twice, and—at the risk of sounding like a travel agent on commission—I have to say those trips have been the most significant weeks of my life thus far. It's hard to even wrap words around the experiences we had. Sailing across the Sea of Galilee, watching the surface of the water change from calm to whitecapped in a matter of minutes. (I would've begged Jesus to calm the storm if I'd been in the boat with Him, too.) Sitting on the Mount of Beatitudes, contemplating what Jesus said on that very hill in His Sermon on the Mount. It was as if the black and white words in our Bibles turned Technicolor and started jumping up off the page! Everywhere we looked we saw a living stage on which some familiar drama in Scripture had once played out.

The Contest on Carmel

One of the most picturesque places we visited was Mount Carmel, the site of an exciting, Oscar-worthy Old Testament story.

The first thing we noticed when the tour bus rumbled to the top of the mountain was an impressive and imposing, fifteen-foot marble statue of Elijah with his sword raised over his head and a terrified man under his faux foot. Elijah's name literally means "the Lord is my God," and his life was packed full of stories that reflected the power of the Lord his God. The monument on Mount Carmel commemorates the grandest story of them all—a battle that took place on that mountain thousands of years ago.

If there was a bookie in that boisterous crowd of onlookers, he probably wasn't getting too many bets on Elijah! The guys in the black hats seemed destined to defeat him. But this battle belonged to the

UNDERDOG

—better yet, to the underdog's Master.

It was the culmination of a series of clashes between Elijah the prophet, God's messenger to the people of Israel, and King Ahab and Queen Jezebel, who jeered Elijah for worshiping Jehovah and bowed down instead to Baal and Asherah (the Canaanite false gods of storm, rain, and fertility). This very carnal king and queen encouraged their subjects to forsake the God of their forefathers and pledge their allegiance to ridiculous rock "deities." Many did, following their rulers into perverse religious practices. Finally the real God told Elijah to challenge the country's false prophets to a "winner takes all" contest on Mount Carmel.

When [Ahab] saw Elijah, he said to him, "Is that you, you troubler of Israel?"

"I have not made trouble for Israel," Elijah replied. "But you and your father's family have. You have abandoned the LORD's commands and have followed the Baals. Now summon the people from all over Israel to meet me on Mount Carmel. And bring four hundred and fifty prophets of Baal and the four hundred prophets of Asherah, who eat at Jezebel's table."

So Ahab sent word throughout all Israel and assembled the prophets on Mount Carmel. Elijah went before the people and said, "How long will you waver between two opinions? If the LORD is God, follow him; but if Baal is God, follow him."

But the people said nothing.

Then Elijah said to them, "I am the only one of the LORD's prophets left, but Baal has four hundred and fifty prophets. Get two bulls for us. Let them choose one for themselves, and let them cut it into pieces and put it on the wood but not set fire to it. I will prepare the other bull and put it on the wood but not set fire to it. Then you will call upon the name of your god, and I will call upon the name of the LORD. The god who answers by fire—he is God."

Then all the people said, "What you say is good." (1 Kings 18:17-24)

Wow, what a dramatic and lopsided duel! There were four hundred and fifty zealots who were bonkers for Baal on one side, and a single Jewish preacher committed to the God of Israel on the other. If there was a bookie in that boisterous crowd of onlookers, he probably wasn't getting too many bets on Elijah! The guys in the black hats seemed destined to defeat him. But this battle belonged to the underdog—better yet, to the underdog's Master:

Elijah said to the prophets of Baal, "Choose one of the bulls and prepare it first, since there are so many of you. Call on the name of your god, but do not light the fire." So they took the bull given them and prepared it.

Then they called on the name of Baal from morning till noon. "O Baal, answer us!" they shouted. But there was no response; no one answered. And they danced around the altar they had made.

At noon Elijah began to taunt them. "Shout louder!" he said. "Surely he is a god! Perhaps he is deep in thought, or busy, or traveling. Maybe he is sleeping and must be awakened." So they shouted louder and slashed themselves with swords and spears, as was their custom, until their blood flowed. Midday passed, and they continued their frantic prophesying until the time for the evening sacrifice. But there was no response, no one answered, no one paid attention....

At the time of sacrifice, the prophet Elijah stepped forward and prayed: "O LORD, God of Abraham, Isaac and Israel, let it be known today that you are God in Israel and that I am your servant and have done all these things at your command. Answer me, O LORD, answer me, so these people will know that you, O LORD, are God, and that you are turning their hearts back again."

Then the fire of the LORD fell and burned up the sacrifice, the wood, the stones and the soil, and also licked up the water in the trench.

When all the people saw this, they fell prostrate and cried, "The LORD—he is God! The LORD—he is God!"

Then Elijah commanded them, "Seize the prophets of Baal. Don't let anyone get away!" They seized them, and Elijah had them brought down to the Kishon Valley and slaughtered there. (1 Kings 18:25–29, 36–40)

When was the last time you "fell prostrate"—at least in your heart—because you were so overwhelmed by God's awesomeness?

Heroes Who Hide

Hooray! Chalk one up for the good guys! In this epitome of "good versus evil," God obliterated the competition, and the people of Israel realized that He was the only God with a capital G.

The carnage on Mount Carmel influenced the Israelites to stop worshiping man-made idols and turn back to their Creator and Redeemer. And God's messenger, the beleaguered yet brave prophet Elijah, went down in Jewish history as a hero. That's why there's a fifteen-foot statue commemorating his exploits on top of that ancient battleground. But the statue doesn't tell the whole story.

> Now Ahab told Jezebel everything Elijah had done and how he had killed all the prophets with a sword. So Jezebel sent a messenger to Elijah to say, "May the gods deal with me, be it ever so severely, if by this time tomorrow I do not make your life like that of one of them."
> Elijah was afraid and ran for his life. When he came to Beersheba in Judah, he left his servant there, while he himself went a day's journey into the desert. He came to a broom tree, sat down under it and prayed that he might die. "I have had enough, LORD," he said. "Take my life; I am no better than my ancestors." (1 Kings 19:1–4)

In light of God's very recent and amazing display of power, doesn't it seem as if Elijah should've laughed in Jezebel's Phoenician face? He'd just witnessed the greatest miracle since the parting of the Red Sea, not to mention all the other miracles he'd seen firsthand prior to the Carmel competition (see 1 Kings 17 for the short list). One big-mouthed woman couldn't be nearly as threatening as hundreds of lunatics waving swords around, and God made mincemeat out of *them*.

But our hero's memory must have been spotty, because he still fell prey to the queen's harassment. Frankly, I don't think the term "hero" fits Elijah at all. I think he was very human. Although he was anointed and appointed by God, he was sometimes weak and sometimes faithless. Not unlike those of us who don't have marble memorials in our honor.

Are there any jeering Jezebels in your life who sometimes harass you into hopelessness?

Broom trees are a rarity in Nashville, but pity parties aren't, and I can certainly empathize with Elijah's depression in the desert. The phrase "I've had enough, Lord" has also echoed through my mind with embarrassing consistency. As a matter of fact, that whiny refrain fell out of my mouth just a few weeks ago, prompted by an irksome house-remodeling project.

Broom trees are a rarity in Nashville, but pity parties aren't, and I can certainly empathize with Elijah's depression in the desert. The phrase "I'VE HAD ENOUGH, LORD" has also echoed through my mind with embarrassing consistency.

Let me set the stage for you. Three years ago I bought a small cottage in a wonderful, old neighborhood full of quaint homes. That's when I learned that "quaint" is often synonymous with "tiny," "overpriced," and "needs a lot of work." So, wielding the clout of a Home Depot credit card, I have become the proud owner of an assortment of power tools. And with the help of my parents and a few friends, I have done lots of "restoration" (and not nearly enough "resting") since buying this place.

The goal of my latest project was pretty ambitious: replace the fifty-year-old, leaky French windows with new ones; replace a wall-sized window with French doors; build steps; break up some asphalt; and lay a flagstone patio—along with a little landscaping in the down time! Thankfully, my sweet mom, Patti, and stepdad, John, traveled all the way from Central Florida to take part in this marathon of do-it-yourself pain.

After the first day of work, however, John came down with a bad case of the flu, which left mom and me holding the hammers. Did I mention that he petered out after cutting out the huge window and leaving a hole in the living room? And this wasn't your ordinary homeowner's hole, either. It was seven feet high, ten feet wide, and three feet off the ground—and conveniently located on the *front* of my house. It turned the living room into an interesting sort of "display case" (kind of like those terrariums we made in elementary school!). Anyone who happened to drive by could amuse themselves by watching our family dynamics through the gaping hole.

It was the middle of August, during one of the worst heat waves in years. As a result, great gusts of air-conditioning from my house were now cooling off the great outdoors. Heavy with grief and half-crazed from the humidity, I turned the thermostat up to ninety degrees so I wouldn't have to take out a loan to pay my electric bill.

The next day, in a burst of Tylenol-fueled energy, John removed one of the bedroom windows but then couldn't get the replacement to fit. After a few choice words, he stumbled back to collapse on the couch (in the middle of the display case), leaving a second, smaller hole on the front of the house to complement the first, more cavernous one. Of course, at that moment it began to rain in torrents, so mom and I scrambled around frantically trying to cover the holes with sheets of plastic and beach towels.

Soon after the tsunami subsided, I raced to the airport to pick up my brother and sister-in-law who, along with their two-year-old son, had flown in for a visit. I was really looking forward to some quality family time and had imagined team charades, barbecues, and group hugs. However, my house only has two small bedrooms and one petite bathroom. Add six people and some pretty big holes in the wall, and pretty soon we were all struggling with grouchiness brought on by rain, mud, heat, and claustrophobia.

I didn't think things could get much worse until I wrecked my best friend's car a few days later. I had just borrowed Kim's SUV for yet another Home Depot run when I crunched into the big blue front end of a car poking out into the intersection where I was turning left. I quickly jumped out of Kim's car and ran to the other driver to make sure she was okay—I assumed she was because it was such a mild fender bender—but when I got to her window, she started complaining about how her neck hurt and how she'd better not get out of the car until an ambulance showed up. Needless to say, I think she'd seen one too many TV commercials about lawyers. A crowd (which included several members of the church where I'm on staff) had gathered by the time she was wheeled off on a stretcher in a neck brace. Meanwhile, I stood forlornly by the policeman, looking every bit the common criminal. I fought the urge to tell the crowd that I hadn't had an accident or a ticket in ten years. I even get the good driver's discount on my insurance policy (well, I used to, anyway).

In the face of Elijah's whining, his crying for relief, and his half-hearted suicide threat, GOD WAS MERCIFUL. *The Creator knows the breaking point of His creations. Instead of a reprimand, He gave Elijah a reprieve.*

Several days later, after my family had gone back to Florida and I was finally alone in my holey house, I sat down with a sigh. I didn't know whether to crawl in bed and pull the covers over my head or just collapse and cry my eyes out. If there had been a broom tree anywhere nearby, I certainly would've crawled under it and told God that I'd had enough.

When was the last time you reached the end of your rope and told God you just couldn't take anymore?

Trembling Followers, Tender Father

When Elijah couldn't take it anymore, he ran away and hid from his problems. And God's response to his fear and frail faith might surprise you. The Alpha and Omega could've chosen to fry Elijah's fanny with a small spark from the fire that barbecued Baal's buddies on Mount Carmel. He could've chastised Elijah and demoted him from prophet emeritus to prophet embarrassed-us. But in the face of Elijah's whining, his crying for relief, and his half-hearted suicide threat, God was merciful. The Creator knows the breaking point of His creations. Instead of a reprimand, He gave Elijah a reprieve. Our gracious heavenly Father gave His weary messenger exactly what he needed: two long naps and some nourishing snacks.

> "I have had enough, LORD," he said. "Take my life; I am no better than my ancestors." Then he lay down under the tree and fell asleep.
>
> All at once an angel touched him and said, "Get up and eat." He looked around, and there by his head was a cake of bread baked over hot coals, and a jar of water. He ate and drank and then lay down again.
>
> The angel of the LORD came back a second time and touched him and said, "Get up and eat, for the journey is too much for you." So he got up and ate and drank. (1 Kings 19:4–8)

And that's not all. God did so much more than just fortify this tired man with warm rolls and good rest. After giving His prophet a refreshing time-out, God sent Elijah on a trip to the mountains, where He personally delivered a message of encouragement:

> The LORD said, "Go out and stand on the mountain in the presence of the LORD, for the LORD is about to pass by."
> Then a great and powerful wind tore the mountains apart and shattered the rocks before the LORD, but the LORD was not in the wind. After the wind there was an earthquake, but the LORD was not in the earthquake. After the earthquake came a fire, but the LORD was not in the fire. And after the fire came a gentle whisper. When Elijah heard it, he pulled his cloak over his face and went out and stood at the mouth of the cave.
> Then a voice said to him, "What are you doing here, Elijah?" (1 Kings 19:11–13)

Isn't it interesting that God chose to speak to Elijah in a *gentle whisper?* He could've thundered and roared some divine decree, since Elijah seemed to need some pointers on perseverance. But He showed tender restraint once more in His message. The Creator of the Universe whispered to one of His whimpering children. Instead of chastising Elijah, God comforted him with His great love.

Have you ever sensed God whispering to your heart?

Last year I met a woman named Molly who has every "right" to curl up and cry. She and her husband had been busy working full-time in college ministry, raising kids, and trying to get by financially. Then their world was rocked by a surprise pregnancy—and their unexpected, beautiful baby boy was born with Down syndrome. I met Molly at a weekend retreat and was struck by her peaceful personality as she carried her precious little guy around the hotel. But when she talked about God's amazing grace and sovereignty in their situation, she also confessed she was tired. Because while the past year had been full of God's providence, it had also been full of constant care and sleepless nights.

After hearing Molly's story, I couldn't stop thinking about her and her family. So when she asked me to sign a book for her at the end of the retreat, I told her I'd be delighted to. While I was writing, however, several people kept talking to me, and in my distracted state I accidentally wrote the wrong word in the front of the book. Flustered, I desperately tried to think of a scripture that included my "wayward word" so I wouldn't have to scribble it out and deface the book before it had even been opened. Then suddenly I remembered a verse with the "mistake word" in it that I could use in the inscription. Breathing a sigh of relief, I handed the book back to Molly and hugged her, wishing I could spend time with her instead of the Chatty Cathys who had me cornered in the lobby.

Molly left, but about ten or fifteen minutes later she emerged from the elevator with a tear-stained face and asked if we could talk. She said she just had to come back to tell me how God had restored her hope through the words I'd written in the front of her book. She explained that the scripture I scribbled was the "life verse" she'd chosen in college but hadn't thought of in a long time. When she opened the book in the elevator on the way to her room, she was stunned. She couldn't believe that out of all the verses I could've written, I chose such an obscure one—yet one that God had engraved deep on her heart almost twenty years before. She was convinced my choice wasn't a coincidence; it was the breath of God reminding her of His faithfulness.

I told Molly that it really was a miracle. I wasn't trying to pick an inspirational passage; I was just trying to cover up a mistake! God used my distracted penmanship as a conduit for compassion and turned a hotel elevator into a hallowed sanctuary in order to refresh one of His children with His relentless love. I got to eavesdrop while God whispered endearments to His exhausted daughter.

I was going through some pictures from Israel the other day, and I paused at the one of Elijah's grand statue. I grinned, thinking about how our proud Jewish guide had frowned in disapproval when I began teaching our tour group about Elijah and his human failings there on top of Mount Carmel. Most religious Jews regard Elijah as one of the greatest Old Testament prophets. His reputation is right up there with Abraham, Moses, and David. But I relate to him much more in his failure than his fame. I'm so glad Scripture records Elijah's broom-tree bellyaching, because God's response reminds me that He is faithful, even when "heroes" are faithless. And that gives my faint heart hope.

By the way, Molly's little boy is also named Elijah.

Focusing on His Faithfulness

1. Have you ever had a "Mount Carmel" season when it seemed that everything was going your way and you felt like a hero? If so, how long did it last? What happened when it was over?

   _____

   _____

   _____

   _____

   _____

2. Who's the meanest, most intimidating "Jezebel" in your life right now? How does he or she affect your life?

_____

_____

_____

_____

_____

_____

_____

_____

3. Describe the last time you reached the end of your metaphorical rope. What was the "broom tree" you crawled under? Describe your experience.

_____

_____

_____

_____

_____

_____

_____

4. How has God "whispered" hope in the midst of your whimpering?

_____

_____

_____

_____

_____

5. Read Psalm 62 and once again memorize and/or post key verses. Write a key verse below.

_____

_____

_____

_____

_____

_____

_____

_____

He can do nothing with the man who thinks that he is of use to God.

—Oswald Chambers

THE PERILS OF
PRETENSE

When I was a little girl, I had three heroes: Samson, Evel Knievel, and Pocahontas. And since Pocahontas was the only girl in the bunch, she was the one I emulated the most. You probably remember her story. She was the famous Indian princess who befriended the English colonists when they settled in Virginia in the early 1600s. When her father, the powerful chief Powhatan, decreed that one of those colonists—a man named John Smith— must die, she threw herself between Smith and his would-be executioners and saved his life.

Pocahontas is credited not only with rescuing John Smith, but also with initiating peace (at least a tenuous one) between the colonists and the natives. Eventually she fell in love and married a distinguished English gentleman, John Rolfe, and they had a little boy named Thomas. Sadly, she died of smallpox a few years later when she was just twenty-one. Although her life was brief, Pocahontas is still remembered for her great bravery and kindness to the early American settlers.

When I was in elementary school—long before Disney portrayed her as a bombshell in buckskin—I wanted to be just like Pocahontas. I begged Mom for a pair of knee-high moccasins and all things beaded so that I could pass for a modern-day warrior woman. Dad even bought me a knife in a leather sheath and a pair of buckskin chaps for riding my horse, Gypsy. I spent most Saturdays on Gypsy's back, riding through the woods pretending to be an Indian princess. Regretfully, we don't have any pictures or home movies that commemorate my Pocahontas period. But I like to think that she would've been proud of my commitment to her memory!

Despite my fervent Pocahontas portrayal, however, I couldn't grow up and be just like her. I wasn't born in the seventeenth century, my dad isn't an important Indian chief, and I've never been patient enough for cross-stitching, much less beadwork. Although I was quite serious at playacting, the reality was that I was just a little ADD Caucasian girl, born in the 1960s, who was pretending to be a brave Indian princess!

My childhood memory of playing "let's pretend" has probably triggered one of your own. I bet you have a sheepish smile on your face right now as you think about it! Because playing a part in a make-believe drama is a normal expression of children's imaginations. Most of us find it endearing to watch a new generation of little ones pretending to be superheroes or cartoon characters. My best friend's four-year-old is quite convinced that he is indeed Spiderman this week! When adults pretend to be someone other than who they are, however, it's not endearing at all. Unless they're making their living on stage, in a soap opera, or on the big screen, inauthentic grownups come across as sad and superficial.

So far we've spent five chapters looking at individuals whose pain, weakness, or failure illuminated God's faithfulness: Hosea, the long-suffering husband of an adulterous woman; Hannah, the heart-broken woman longing for a child; the crippled man who couldn't get into the water by himself; Balaam, the psychic who couldn't see God's directions clearly; and Elijah, who got scared and ran for his life. But now we're going to take the next two chapters to look at *groups* of people who demonstrate spiritual slowness.

Big Daddies of Decorum

The Pharisees were a very dimwitted group when it came to the Deity. Yet they played the part of religious leaders better than any-body. Flourishing during the first century B.C. and the first century A.D.—which means they were prominent during the time of Jesus' earthly ministry—they elevated make-believe to an art form. They were largely comprised of legalistic laymen who sought to apply the Torah (the Jewish book of wisdom and law that now makes up most of our Old Testament canon) to every facet of life. They spent a great deal of their time hanging out in the synagogues, hunched over copies of the Law and the "oral traditions" they wrote in order to interpret the six hundred or so biblical precepts. They used these oral traditions, or interpretations, to enforce rigid behavioral guide-lines among the common people.

The majority of Jewish people were "regular Joes," just trying to eke out a living as farmers or shepherds. The term for these people was *Am ha-Eretz*, which literally means "the people of the land."[1] Most men and certainly all women and children among the Am ha-Eretz were illiterate. And since they couldn't read the Torah for themselves, they had to trust the Pharisees to interpret it for them.

Of course the prideful Pharisees were thrilled to be the liaisons between the Jewish people and Jehovah. And they were oh-so-picky about creating and enforcing the parameters for proper behavior. Their debates centered on issues such as what type of food you could or couldn't eat. How to cut your hair. How to bandage skin ailments. When you could or couldn't be physically intimate with your marriage partner. They were passionate about policies—but clueless about a personal relationship with the Prince of Peace.

Does that description fit any picky church people you know? Have you ever been more concerned about following spiritual "rules" or fulfilling religious responsibilities than you were with pursuing an intimate personal relationship with Jesus Christ?

The Pharisees' preoccupation with religious regulations and the oppressive way they enforced their beliefs on the common people infuriated Jesus. Instead of demonstrating brokenness and repentance, they were the epitome of spiritual pride. And on several very public occasions, He rebuked them for their pretense. One of the most dramatic dressing-downs is recorded in Matthew, and it was during this lecture (commonly referred to as the "Seven Woes") that Jesus accused the Pharisees of being the great pretenders. He reprimanded them for pretending to love God but not practicing what they preached. Here are three of the "woes" Jesus used to expose their deceit and duplicity:

> Woe to you, teachers of the law and Pharisees, you hypocrites! You shut the kingdom of heaven in men's faces. You yourselves do not enter, nor will you let those enter who are trying to....
>
> Woe to you, teachers of the law and Pharisees, you hypocrites! You clean the outside of the cup and dish, but inside they are full of greed and self-indulgence. Blind Pharisee! First clean

the inside of the cup and dish, and then the outside also will be clean.

Woe to you, teachers of the law and Pharisees, you hypocrites! You are like whitewashed tombs, which look beautiful on the outside but on the inside are full of dead men's bones and everything unclean. In the same way, on the outside you appear to people as righteous but on the inside you are full of hypocrisy and wickedness. (Matthew 23:13, 25–28)

Oscar-Worthy Arrogance

Yikes! They must've been so embarrassed! To say that "Jesus stepped on their toes" with this stinging judgment is a huge understatement. The Pharisees weren't just upset about His confrontational comments; they were furious enough to start planning His murder. And the word He used that probably fueled their anger to the boiling point was *hypocrite*.

Hypocrite is a term found only in the Gospels of Matthew, Mark, and Luke, and it's only spoken through the lips of Jesus. No one else in the entirety of the Holy Writ ever uses the word *hypocrite*. It goes without saying that Jesus is the only One worthy of calling someone else such a thing. Because *hypocrite* is a Greek word that means "stage-actor"[2]—and Jesus used this theatrical terminology to accuse the Pharisees of some serious spiritual make-believe!

He probably couldn't have found a word that would have been more offensive to their egotistical ears, because the Pharisees thought that actors were the vilest of men. You see, theater was a Greek phenomenon, and religious Jews were horrified by everything Greek. Yet they were surrounded by it on all sides. As a result of the Greek conquests (followed by the Romans, who adopted the Greek way of life) throughout the Middle East, Greek (or "Hellenistic") culture had become the norm in most civilized nations, including Israel.

To the Pharisees' horror, these cheeky Greeks and Romans violated the laws of the Torah in every way, shape, and form. Instead of worshiping Jehovah, the one true God, they practiced *polytheism*, which means they worshiped "many gods." They also threw a pinch of astronomy and astrology into their belief system for good measure. They were moral and religious anarchists whose basic creed was "If it feels good, do it!"

And the theater was the centerpiece of their lascivious lifestyle. Many Greek plays featured full nudity, with actors engaging in all kinds of pornographic activity. Even modern movie critics would have blushed at some of their plot lines. So for Jesus to call the religious leaders of His day "hypocrites" or "actors" was a scandalous characterization! He insulted these important religious men in the worst possible way. Can you imagine waltzing up to your pastor's wife next Sunday and loudly calling her a prostitute? I'm sure an electric wave of stunned disbelief would circulate through your congregation in seconds! The expressions Jesus used to denounce the Pharisees were no less shocking. No one had ever spoken to these men like that before. So why did He?

I think the Son of God expressed righteous anger toward the Pharisees because their pretentious performance made a mockery of the Gospel. They insisted on following a formula instead of repenting and putting their faith in the forgiveness and mercy of God. Their dangerous game of pious make-believe led others to believe that they could never approach God, much less be loved by Him. After all, who could possibly check off every single box of appropriate religious behavior?

It's probably important to note that not all Pharisees were "bad" men; Nicodemus and Joseph of Arimathea were both Pharisees, and they are portrayed positively in the Gospels. The truth is, the Pharisees' beliefs weren't completely *wrong*; they were completely *offtrack*. They believed in angels, an afterlife, and a Messiah (just not Jesus!). But their emphasis on legalistic minutia missed the point and pointed others in the wrong direction. Their acting skills were admirable, but their religion was one of meaningless mechanics. Cloaking themselves in the facade of having all the answers to life's spiritual questions, they created the criteria for

This precious older woman was sincere in

HER BELIEF

that I was headed for you-know-where because of my dress code.

appropriate religious behavior based on those "answers" and built hypocritical hoops people had to jump through in order to be admitted into their "God squad."

Sadly, our churches are still full of people who monitor others based on a legalistic list of "approved" Christian activities. As a matter of fact, I came face to face with one recently. A well-dressed woman came up to me at the end of a retreat where I was teaching and said, "I was really surprised to find out you were the speaker at the beginning of the weekend. I thought you were one of those non-Christians we were supposed to invite so they could be saved."

Her forthright comments tickled me, so I asked her why she assumed I wasn't a Christian. She hesitated for a few seconds and then said, "Well, I noticed you were wearing chunky shoes and dark lipstick at registration. I expected a Bible teacher to look more conservative."

Now, I may have missed something in my doctrinal digging, but I have yet to come upon a scripture that mandates stodgy shoes and pale lipstick for believers! Yet this precious older woman was sincere in her belief that I was headed for you-know-where because of my dress code. If I wanted a part in her spiritual play, I needed to go back to the wardrobe room—because I definitely didn't look spiritual enough! She had a clear case of Pharisee fever. And like the Pharisees, she will have missed the main point of the Gospel if she continues to think that God cares more about the thickness of our shoe soles than the condition of our spiritual ones.

What do you think a Christian should look like? Do you have some unwritten rules for how you think believers should dress or behave?

Big Boxes and Battered Bibles

Like the fashion policewoman at the retreat, the Pharisees were very preoccupied with appearance. They were much more concerned with *looking* spiritual than they were with loving God with all their hearts and loving their neighbors as themselves. In another one of His verbal missiles aimed right at the heart of their arrogance, Jesus points this out: "Everything they do is done for men to see: They make their phylacteries wide and the tassels on their garments long; they love the place of honor at banquets and the most important seats in the synagogues; they love to be greeted in the marketplaces and to have men call them 'Rabbi'" (Matthew 23:5–7).

The *phylacteries* Jesus referred to were strips of parchment—or wooden boxes containing the parchment—that the Pharisees wore on their foreheads and their hands (and sometimes on their left arms, in order to place them close to their hearts).[3] These parchments commemorated God's commands in Exodus and Deuteronomy to love

Him "with all your heart and with all your soul and with all your strength" (Exodus 13:3–16; Deuteronomy 6:4–9; 11:13–21). God wanted His people to remember to keep His commands and fear Him, so He told them, "Fix these words of mine in your hearts and minds; tie them as symbols on your hands and bind them on your foreheads" (Deuteronomy 11:19).

The long tassels Jesus referred to were worn by the Pharisees in adherence to Numbers 15:37–40, a passage in which God tells the Israelites to wear tassels with blue cords on the corners of their robes—again with the intent of encouraging them to remember His commands and obey Him. In other words, the tassels and the phylacteries were *symbols* by which God's people were to remember His Word. But instead of humbly committing themselves to reverent remembrance, the Pharisees missed God's point. They got hung up on trying to *look* spiritual. They became consumed with seeing who could strap the biggest, most beautiful box on his head and who could make his fringes the fluffiest!

I don't have a hard time picturing a bunch of stuffy men parading around with boxes on their heads and hands and tassels trailing behind them, because a few sects of Judaism still practice those rituals today. On my two trips to Israel, they were hard to miss. The first time I saw the "box and tassel" bunch, I was with a group of women in the Newark, New Jersey, airport, waiting to board our flight to Israel. We were giddy with excitement about our trip to the Holy Land, and none of us had gotten much sleep the night before. So we were laughing and talking and trading candy and magazines, while these very serious-looking men with long beards; long, curly sideburns; long, black coats; protruding phylacteries; and bobbing, blue fringe kept glancing at us with stern disapproval.

85

I wasn't intimidated by them as much as I was intrigued. They were the first Hasidic Jewish men I'd ever seen up close. And I really wanted to talk to them because I'd recently taken a class in Jewish history and had come away with a deep respect for their heritage and culture.

I thought it was pure providence, therefore, that our tour group of twenty-five chatty Christian women ended up being seated right next to the beard-and-black-coat section for the entire twelve-hour flight to Tel Aviv. I smiled at the men while we were stuffing our bags into the overhead bins and getting situated. But I never got to talk to them or ask them any questions. As a matter of fact, they made it quite clear that they would *not* talk to any of us. They walked back and forth through the aisles at least a dozen times for ritual prayers or to smoke in the back of the plane. But they pointedly ignored us with every passing. When I attempted a polite greeting, I was rebuffed with undisguised scorn. The closest they ever came to acknowledging us was to whip their fringe across our sleeping faces as they swept by to recite more prayers, reeking of stale cigarettes. And let me tell you, being whacked in the eyeball with a big, blue tassel in the middle of the night on a long smoking flight is not enjoyable!

Needless to say, by the end of our twelve hours together, I wasn't the least bit impressed with their spiritual appearance. At the end of the flight, they butted in front of us to deplane first—nearly tripping one of the elderly women in our group—and I found myself thinking that they were probably a lot like the Pharisees whom Jesus scolded so severely in the Seven Woes. Although they never missed a prayer on the plane, they didn't reflect any of the compassion of the God they were supposedly praying to. Their wardrobes were replete with dangling reminders of God's Word, but their hearts seemed to have long forgotten His mercy. Not only had they missed the Messiah, they didn't even reflect joy in their rigid devotion to Jehovah. The play these modern religious "actors" performed was a tragedy.

Pharisee Perfume

But we have to be careful not to judge these religious Jews too harshly. Gentiles can't afford to gloat, because our community is bloated with Pharisees, too. I've never worn a literal box on my head or hands, but I've sure struggled with some metaphorical boxes and floppy fringe.

I remember reeking of Pharisee perfume at a Christian conference a few years ago. I had misplaced the Bible I've used since high school and had to take another one to this particular event. I was the youngest, least-known speaker on the platform, so I was already a little nervous sitting next to the really "important" people in the evangelical community. And as I clutched my barely-been-used Bible, I started getting more nervous, worrying about what they might think. My new Bible had crisp, unmarked pages—even the most familiar passages like John 3:16 hadn't been underlined yet!—and I was afraid the other speakers might glance over, see those pristine pages, and decide that I must not be a very "deep" Christian! *If only I had my old, tattered Bible*, I thought. Because somewhere in my insecure soul, I reasoned that duct tape on the binding and multicolored highlighting on the pages would be proof of my spirituality. I wanted to *look* spiritual, and my penchant for well-worn Bibles was every bit as Pharisaic as the quest for ten-foot tassels.

What about you? What are the metaphorical phylacteries or tassels you "wear" in order to look more spiritual?

One of our consistent prayers should be for God to reveal the hypocrite in our hearts. We need to purge our inner Pharisee—our concern with *looking* spiritual, our desire to create the criteria for everyone else's behavior, our arrogant tendency to have all the answers, our penchant to perform meaningless religious rituals. Following a set of man-made rules isn't the key to eternal life; faith in Christ is. We receive salvation because of God's mercy and faithfulness toward us, not because of anything we do or say or wear. Bigger boxes, longer tassels, and raggedy Bibles don't represent righteousness. Our righteousness is based solely on the substitutionary sacrifice of Jesus Christ. And when we meet Him as our personal Messiah and experience His redemptive love, there's no need to play make-believe anymore.

Focusing on His Faithfulness

1. Why do you think following "religious rules" makes most people feel more secure and justified in their faith?

_____

_____

_____

_____

_____

_____

2. Describe what you think a stereotypical Christian looks like.

_____

_____

_____

_____

_____

_____

_____

3. What are some examples of things you *wear*, *say*, or *do* mainly to impress others with your "spirituality"?

_____

_____

_____

_____

_____

_____

_____

4. Read the entire chapter of Matthew 23. Do any of the "Seven Woes" describe you? How?

_____

_____

_____

_____

_____

_____

_____

5. Spend time alone in prayer and ask God to reveal the hypocrite in your heart. Write here what he reveals.

_____

_____

_____

_____

_____

_____

_____

_____

6. Prayerfully consider asking your spouse or a close friend to tell you honestly about any hypocritical areas he or she has noticed in your life. Write what this person might point out.

_____

_____

_____

_____

_____

_____

_____

_____

Grace is not simply leniency when we have sinned. Grace is the enabling gift of God not to sin. Grace is power, not just pardon.

—John Piper

BARGAIN-BASEMENT
GRACE

I went through a mini-midlife crisis last year and became the proud owner of a black motorcycle. My insurance premiums shot up, along with a few church eyebrows. Especially when I wore my leather pants. Let me tell you, there are a few modern-day Pharisees in Nashville who are horrified by the sight of a female, leather-wearing Bible teacher on a motorcycle. And I have to admit that part of me enjoys bucking convention and bending the rules a bit!

There weren't any motorcycle mamas roaring around—I'm not sure about the leather pants part—but there were definitely people who bent the rules during the apostle Paul's era, too. One particularly rebellious group rejected *all* of the religious rules the Pharisees held so dear. They were at the other end of the spiritual spectrum from the stiff guys we talked about in the last chapter. They were known as the "antinomians," which is a Greek word meaning "against the law." And even though their beliefs were the polar opposite of the Pharisees, they also missed the main point of the Gospel and were just as far offtrack. The Book of Jude refers to them when it says, "They are godless men, who change the grace of our God into a license for immorality" (Jude 4).

Rebels without a Clue

While lots of religious people objected to Paul's teaching, the antinomians loved it—particularly his emphasis on divine grace being the only path to salvation. They twisted his teaching about the Gospel into an excuse to behave without any regard for biblical boundaries. Sin had no stigma in their bargain-basement version of grace, which absolved them from any responsibility for their actions. Paul challenged the idiocy of their ideas in his letter to the Romans, and although about two thousand years have passed, his comments remain right on target. Because our culture is still full of New Age antinomians devoted to bargain-basement grace.

"What shall we say, then?" he wrote in Romans 6:1–2. "Shall we go on sinning so that grace may increase? By no means!"

One of my good friends has a darling four-year-old son who is typically very well behaved, but who is also very much a little boy—and as such, has become enthralled with picking his nose. My friend wasn't nearly as horrified about his habit as I was when it first started. She is an even-tempered "boy" mom who knew it would just be a matter of time before he quit. Thinking she was way too calm about this calamity, I decided to help him break the nasty habit when I rode along with them on a three-hour car trip.

Summoning all my creative energy, I made up a little rhyming song that listed all the reasons why children *shouldn't* pick their noses! He was delighted with the tune and tapped his feet along with the beat. He even started singing the "Naughty Nose" song along with me! I was excited that he was being so attentive and assumed he would stop the revolting ritual immediately. Especially since I had taken the time to make the lesson on good manners so fun and interactive. But he didn't stop at all. Becoming the center of my attention encouraged him to continue his tacky habit with gusto!

His toddler philosophy is similar to that of the grace-abusers. Antinomians reasoned that the more flagrantly they sinned, the more grace would flourish. And although that ancient logic sounds ludicrous to most of us, people have been deceived by it throughout history. Third-century records tell of devout Christian martyrs, ultimately killed for their faith in Christ, who devoted their last nights in prison to drunken binges and promiscuity because they'd bought into such thinking. Rasputin, the infamous Russian monk who greatly influenced Emperor Nicholas II around the turn of the twentieth century, encouraged his followers to sin with passion so they'd receive more grace.

But possibly the most interesting example of intentional sinning took place in seventeenth-century England among an extremist religious sect known as the *Ranters*. The Ranters' doctrine was based on their belief in the "holiness of sin." They embraced the concept that believers were made perfect by God's indwelling Spirit; thus, they had complete license to do whatever they felt like. Two of their more eyebrow-raising hobbies were wife swapping and parading around in the nude. One of their leaders was even said to have cussed for a solid hour behind a pulpit in London. I bet no one fell asleep in church that Sunday!

Although I'm not aware of any "Ranters" in modern evangelical circles, the same distortion of grace is still a huge problem. Our churches are packed full of people who smile and shake hands in shiny clothes on Sunday, only to resume lying, cheating, and gossiping at the office on Monday. Much like the Ranters, many religious people today think the whole concept of sin is too restrictive. They call themselves "enlightened" and consider a biblical moral code antiquated and irrelevant. Little do they realize that their "new" warped way of thinking is as ancient as a dinosaur fossil!

Is your behavior the same regardless of your environment? Are you the same person around Christians and non-Christians? Or do you tend to rationalize sin based on your surroundings?

The Stench of Sin

Paul's letter to the Romans debunks this distorted doctrine. And he refutes it with style; I really like his colorful use of a life-and-death metaphor to explain that no Christian who has been made alive in Christ should be pining for the grave:

> We died to sin; how can we live in it any longer? Or don't you know that all of us who were baptized into Christ Jesus were baptized into his death? We were therefore buried with him through baptism into death in order that, just as Christ was raised from the dead through the glory of the Father, we too may live a new life. (Romans 6:2–4)

Several years ago I saw a movie called *Rob Roy*, starring Jessica Lange and Liam Neeson. (Don't rent it unless you have a strong stomach!) The movie is liberally based on the true story of a Scotsman named Rob Roy, who led a revolt in the eighteenth century against Scotland's wealthy English landowners. Portrayed as horribly cruel and unjust in their "business tactics," the landowners raped and pillaged and took whatever they wanted from the Scots who worked their land. So Rob Roy attempted to organize the first union to stand up against the "evil elite."

In a particularly vivid scene in the movie, Rob Roy is shown running for his life with a group of men on horseback hot on his trail. He races down a hill and begins searching desperately for a place to hide before his enemies gallop down the slope and find him. And just when you think, *Oh no, they're going to kill him!*—because he's in this big, open field with nowhere to hide—the camera pans to a dead cow in a shallow pond. Quick as a flash, Rob Roy dives into the water, scrapes out the cow's innards, and climbs into the carcass just as the bad guys arrive. They look every which way, twisting and turning in their saddles, and become furious when they realize he has miraculously eluded them.

Although I'm not aware of any "Ranters" in modern evangelical circles, the same DISTORTION OF GRACE is still a huge problem.

Of course, they never go near the water because of the terrible stench. And while everyone in the theater was glad Rob Roy escaped, we were also wincing and wrinkling our noses. It's hard to imagine how anyone could climb into the rotting remains of a dead animal!

That's basically what Paul is communicating in Romans 6, without the benefit of the big screen: "Now that you've experienced the incredible sweetness of new life in Christ, what in the world would possess you to climb into a cadaver?" Paul is kind of like Arnold Schwartzenegger when it comes to the antinomians' agenda of sugar-coating sin. He aims right for the heart of their perverse philosophy and fires away! He mounts a direct attack on their assertion that God doesn't mind our behavior, no matter how reprehensible it is. To him, their distorted Gospel is just as repugnant as Rob Roy's hiding place!

But then he throws his readers a curve ball:

> In the same way, count yourselves dead to sin but alive to God in Christ Jesus. Therefore do not let sin reign in your mortal body so that you may obey its evil desires. Do not offer the parts of your body to sin, as instruments of wickedness, but rather offer yourselves to God, as those who have been brought from death to life; and offer the parts of your body to him as instruments of righteousness. For sin shall not be your master, because you are not under the law, but under grace. (Romans 6:11–14)

Huh? Run that one by us again, Paul, because it sounds like you're changing your tune here! You just told us that we died to sin, that our sinful bodies were crucified with Christ. But now we're not supposed to let sin reign or rule in our bodies. Make up your mind: Is sin dead or not?

I call Romans 6 the "Stay Dead Chapter" because it talks about our struggle with something that should be six feet under! A little later in the letter he expounds on sin's notorious ability to rear its ugly, should-be-dead head when he writes, "I do not understand what I do. For what I want to do I do not do, but what I hate I do…. I know that nothing good lives in me, that is, in my sinful nature. For I have the desire to do what is good, but I cannot carry it out" (Romans 7:15, 18). The somewhat perplexing point Paul makes is that while we are dead to sin's authority, we aren't immune to its temptation. In other words, as Christians, we are dead to sin's *dominion*—it can't separate us from the love of God—but we still live in sin's *domain*. We are free from the penalty of death that accompanies sin, but we are not free from sin's persuasion.

Dallying with Disobedience

Several weeks ago I got a phone call from a friend I hadn't talked to in about a year. I had the opportunity to get to know her and her husband some time ago through a ministry we were all associated with. We spent time together on several trips—skiing in Colorado and swimming in Cancun. We bonded over the Bible and over wearing bathing suits in public! I found them to be a fun, outgoing Christian couple. They were also respected members of their community. She's very involved as a volunteer at their kids' Christian school, and he was elected to a key leadership position in their church. Together they led Bible studies and mission trips and gave generously of both time and money to all sorts of ministries.

So when my friend called and told me about her husband's ongoing affair with another woman and the horrible details that led to their pending divorce, I was shocked. It's hard to picture this man standing on the lawn yelling obscenities in front of his young children, as my friend described. I never would have imagined him saying and doing some of the things she told me. He didn't seem like the type of guy who would turn his back on his family, friends, and faith. All over an illicit love affair with an immoral woman! And he thinks his behavior is justified because, as he says, "I know God wants me to be happy."

I'm praying that God will redeem their marriage. He certainly could. Maybe this husband will have a King David experience and respond to confrontation with brokenness. Maybe he'll miraculously recognize his sin, repent, and run home to his grieving wife and children. But even if this prodigal returns, there will still be con-sequences. His children already have deep wounds as a result of their daddy's selfish and sinful behavior. Sin is never innocuous. It leaves scars. The baby boy Bathsheba gave birth to after her affair with King David died as a result of his daddy's sin. It's sobering to realize that even those who teach Bible studies about the danger and damage caused by sin aren't immune to its allure.

The same **SNAKE** *who tempted Eve with an apple uses even more sophisticated fruit to entice us to veer off God's path.*

Wouldn't it be wonderful if the influence of this insidious thing called sin disappeared the moment we became Christians? It sure would make life easier! Although the multi-billion-dollar porn industry would be in trouble and drug dealers would have to get real jobs. But sin doesn't simply disappear from the radar screen for those of us who've been redeemed. The same snake who tempted Eve with an apple uses even more sophisticated fruit to entice us to veer off God's path.

Sin remains a struggle for us because sanctification—being made holy—is a process, not an immediate "*poof,* now you're holy." We won't be completely free from sin's magnetism until we're in heaven. Earth isn't our true home; and until we're in glory with our heavenly Father, the father of lies will continue to try to lure us away from God. Sometimes my should-be-dead sin nature pops up with such vim and vigor, it's as if a handsome emergency room doctor applied heart paddles and jump-started it!

Bargain-basement grace salesmen will tell you that revived sin natures aren't a big deal. That they're *covered* by God's amazing grace. And they're right—sort of. But again, they miss the main point. Jesus paid the penalty for our sins—past, present, and future—on the cross. As a result of His atoning death, God is swift to redeem us when we repent and ask for His forgiveness. But His grace didn't come at a bargain price. He paid the highest price imaginable by sacrificing His Son. And *repentance* is a military term, which means to do an about-face. To go in the opposite direction. To turn away from the sin that so easily entraps us.

Direct disobedience is a big deal. It literally flies in the face of God's holiness. It pollutes the fellowship we have with Him, not to mention our relationships with others. The apostle Peter wrote, "As obedient children, do not conform to the evil desires you had when you lived in ignorance. But just as he who called you is holy, so be holy in all you do; for it is written: 'Be holy, because I am holy'" (1 Peter 1:14–16).

The Christian writer Dietrich Bonhoeffer called delusional doctrines that leave out the issue of repentance "cheap grace." He said that every conversion includes a call to discipleship. If we believe in the Lord Jesus Christ, then we are also called to look like Him. We are called to Christlikeness.

Do you think the people closest to you would say you "look" like Jesus? What about the people you work and/or socialize with— would they say you resemble your Redeemer?

Visualizing Our Cornerstone

I used to work with a youth ministry, and much of my time was spent with high school girls. My favorite among them was a precious young woman with a heart for God and a spunky spirit. I got to lead a Bible study with "Connie" (not her real name!) and several other girls for three years. We spent countless hours praying and talking, laughing and crying, and grew to love each other like sisters. And as the "big sister" and Bible teacher, I learned to listen at length to their concerns and problems.

Connie's dating dilemmas were usually the most melodramatic of all. She had a hard time separating true love from raging hormones. During her senior year, she started dating a young man whom she was convinced was "the one." They met at a Christian retreat and started leading junior-high Bible studies together. They were such a cute couple. Their delight in each other was practically contagious! But pretty soon they were both infected with the "groping virus." She tearfully confessed their struggles and asked me to help hold her accountable to sexual purity. We prayed about it and looked up Bible verse "boundaries"—all to no avail. Their puppy lust just wouldn't stay dead!

We aren't saved by ignoring our desires and following the "rules," as the Pharisees taught. But pretending that **BIBLICAL BOUNDARIES** *don't matter isn't the answer.*

Finally I told her to start imagining Jesus standing in the corner of the room when they had their "horizontal conferences" on the couch. We talked about the reality of God's presence in our lives and how we'd be less likely to sin if we could literally see Him. I said that maybe *looking for Jesus* would help her to *look more like Him.*

A few nights later the phone woke me up, and Connie's voice was on the other end shrieking, "It worked! It worked!" She said she scared her boyfriend half to death when he laid her back on the couch and started to kiss her, because she sat up and declared that Jesus was right behind him! After visualizing her Savior in the room, Connie didn't feel comfortable with her Romeo's roving hands. She still had a very healthy libido—God doesn't remove our hormones—but the Holy Spirit helped her to stop practicing habitual sin. Sinful behavior became an opponent that she took very seriously. She became wary of its temporary sweetness and learned to guard against its temptation.

Like Connie, we need to guard our hearts from the tempting "treats" that sin offers up to quench our desires. God's love is the only thing that will satisfy our deepest longings.

We aren't saved by ignoring our desires and following the "rules," as the Pharisees taught. But pretending that biblical boundaries don't matter isn't the answer. If we only focus on the law, our hearts won't be transformed; but if we wink at sin like the antinomians, our hearts won't be transformed either. It is only when we recognize the perfect relationship between God's mercy and His holiness, between our repentance and His redemption, that grace really becomes grace.

I'd like to close this chapter with a disclaimer, because I know there are some theological problems with the semantics of "seeing Jesus in the corner." The Bible makes it clear that Jesus resides in us through the Holy Spirit; He takes up residence in our souls, making us "temples of the Holy Spirit" (1 Corinthians 3:16; 2 Corinthians 6:16). He is certainly not some "silent chaperone" standing a few feet away, frowning with disapproval at frisky high school couples!

Still, I think we can all benefit from imagining that Jesus, our merciful Savior, is present in every room—even in the dark corners—of our lives. After all, He promises, "I am with you always" (Matthew 28:20). And that—God's present, abiding, and relentless love—is the only thing that will cause sin to lose its appeal.

Focusing on His Faithfulness

1. If we're dead to sin, why do we still struggle with it?

_____

_____

_____

_____

_____

_____

_____

2. What's the "besetting" sinful behavior in your life—the sin that just won't stay dead? What can you do to "kill" that sin?

_____

_____

_____

_____

_____

_____

3. Describe a time in your life when you were really aware of being "dead to sin"—when you felt like everything in you was "walking in righteousness."

_____

_____

_____

_____

_____

_____

_____

4. Which group do you identify with more, the Pharisees or the antinomians? Why?

_____

_____

_____

_____

_____

_____

_____

_____

5. Read Romans 12. Write down some practical ways in which you can stop conforming to the pattern of the world.

_____

_____

_____

_____

_____

_____

_____

_____

We are to love one another as God has loved us. That is the truth of it. But to love one another more than God has loved us—to love one another at the expense of our own freedom to be something like whole and at peace within ourselves, and at the expense of others' freedom, too—is the dark shadow that the truth casts.

—Frederick Buechner

COMPANY THAT
CORRUPTS

When I was living in Colorado, I asked my Aunt Darlene to hike into the belly of the Grand Canyon with me. I had been there once before, so I enthusiastically described the hike in detail: the amazing red rock formations; the Havasu Indian reservation we'd pass through; the incredible, iridescent blue waterfall at the end of the trail. After listening to my energetic advertisement, she and her husband, Dale, decided that a hike in the Grand Canyon would be a fun addition to their family vacation. Their kids got excited, too, when they were told about their upcoming adventure.

But then Darlene started getting a little nervous about how tax-ing the trip would be physically, especially since Steven and Sarah were only eleven and eight. I assured her the kids would be fine and said the hike wasn't even as difficult as some of the trails she and I had hiked together before.

It had been a few years since I'd hiked the canyon's Havasupai Trail, and I had been in great shape at the time. I honestly didn't remember it being all that strenuous. Since I'd hiked the entire twenty-six mile trail in one day, I figured the two-day trip we were planning would be a breeze! Darlene took my word for it and finalized their vacation details.

A few months later we met up in Flagstaff, Arizona. My friend Sally and I had driven fourteen hours to get there, and Darlene's family had caravaned halfway across the country; so we were all pretty weary before we even started hiking. But we got up before dawn the next morning, carbo-loaded at the local Waffle House, and then high-tailed it to the Havasu Indian Reservation, where the trail begins.

It takes about three hours to drive from Flagstaff to the trail-head, and the last fifty miles are completely barren—no gas stations, no McDonald's, not even a Port-o-Potty. So when we pulled into the dusty parking lot in the middle of nowhere, everyone turned toward me to make sure we were in the right place. Looking around, it was hard to believe we were about to begin a beautiful wilderness experience! But I assured everyone that this was indeed the place and that the hike was going to be easy and exciting.

Parents appeased, children hopping up and down in anticipation, we crammed last-minute supplies into bulging backpacks and began walking down the rocky trail. And for about two hours, the hike was pure honeymoon. The scenery was awe-inspiring, and our spirits soared. But pretty soon the temperature did, too. Then the trail started rising to keep the mercury company! Our happy little troupe turned into a sweaty, bedraggled bunch of tenderfoots. And because of all my "don't worry, it'll be easy" assurances, I was feeling more guilty by the minute.

It was almost eight hours before we finally dragged into camp at the bottom of the Grand Canyon. My friend Sally had been flattened by a runaway horse (horses and mules are the only mode of transportation on the trail, so they run up and down the trail every few hours, loaded with supplies); Darlene's backpack had rubbed blisters into her shoulders; and both children were glassy-eyed with fatigue. We put up the tents so we'd have a place to plop our tired bodies, only to discover that the Army surplus model Darlene had rented was too small for a family of four. Then Sally sat down wearily and pulled off her new hiking boots. At the sight of her bloody socks, we all gasped.

I helped her bandage her tortured toes, then tried to prop up everyone's sagging spirits by leading a trek to the waterfall. But the awesome torrent I remembered had become little more than a trickle because of the summer drought. Just when I thought things couldn't get any worse, Darlene unpacked "dinner." I'd told her to pack granola bars but forgot to tell her not to get the ones covered in chocolate. And string cheese always held up really well on my camping trips in Colorado, so I'd encouraged her to pack a lot of that portable protein. I hadn't stopped to think about what happens to cheese in the desert heat.

Not only was her family's strength totally sapped, now they were going to starve, too! Scooping the melted chocolate and runny cheese out of her backpack was more than Darlene could bear. My outgoing, optimistic aunt hobbled over to a rock, sat down, and began to cry. And I felt like a total creep.

None of us slept that night. I wiggled around in my sandy sleeping bag and worried about being charged with unintentional multiple hiking homicide. Darlene said she listened to unidentifiable nocturnal sounds and worried about how in the world they were going to hike out of the canyon in the morning. She told me that was the first time in her life that she literally prayed for God to save her husband and children from certain death.

We got up before the sun and formed a pitiful procession, shuffling along in the dark. Except for the noise of our hiking boots crunching through sand and rocks, all was silent. The fun family vacation had deteriorated into a death march!

After a few miles, Sally and I had to part ways with Darlene, Dale, and the kids, because we had to hustle to get back to Colorado Springs in order to make it to work on time Monday morning. We felt terrible about leaving, as if we were abandoning a sinking ship. Saying quick goodbyes, we gritted our teeth and gutted out the grueling hike back to the car in three hours, not knowing the same trip would take Darlene's family all day. And what a day it was! By the time they made it to the steepest section of the hike, where the trail winds up the canyon wall, they were completely out of energy and water. Dale collapsed in a skimpy area of shade because he had a mild heatstroke, which Darlene misdiagnosed as a heart attack. She flagged down a stoic Indian on horseback and tearfully begged him to carry Sarah out of the canyon, promising him all the cash in her purse if they made it out. She told me afterward that between fanning her fainting husband and watching her youngest child ride off into the sunset with a total stranger, she despaired of ever making it out alive.

We got up before the sun and formed a **PITIFUL PROCESSION,** *shuffling along in the dark. The fun family vacation had deteriorated into a death march!*

Eventually another stranger stopped and shared some Gatorade, and they were able to limp up the cliff to their car. But when they finally made it back to their hotel room in Flagstaff, Darlene accidentally turned the heat on full blast instead of the air conditioning. And as they lay sprawled on the beds, dripping with perspiration, she thought maybe heatstroke was contagious and that they were now going to meet their Maker in the Marriott! (Thankfully, one of the kids realized her mistake and turned off the heat.) Needless to say, Darlene adamantly refuses to go on another Grand Canyon hike with me. She's decided that letting her guard down once was more than enough. Trusting me again for trail advice would be hazardous to her health!

Samson's Special Delivery

In one of my favorite Bible stories of all times, a marriage-impaired Jewish man also learned that questionable company can be bad for your health. You may remember that Samson is a member of my triad of childhood heroes, and he's the only biblical one of the bunch! Mom says she got so tired of reading his story every night at bedtime that she begged me to pick another one. But Canaan wasn't nearly as captivating, and the Red Sea wasn't as remarkable as the strongest man in the Old Testament, in my opinion. I never wavered in my affection and admiration for Samson during the bedtime story process. I'm not sure why I liked him so much, though. Because even though he was one of the bravest men in Scripture and consistently beat up the bad guys, he was also completely clueless when it came to keeping vows and choosing friends.

Like Isaac and Samuel, Samson was the promised son of a couple who struggled with infertility. An angel appeared twice to announce Samson's arrival and give his parents directions about parenting him:

A certain man of Zorah, named Manoah, from the clan of the Danites, had a wife who was sterile and remained childless. The angel of the LORD appeared to her and said, "You are sterile and childless, but you are going to conceive and have a son. Now see to it that you drink no wine or other fermented drink and that you do not eat anything unclean, because you will conceive and give birth to a son. No razor may be used on his head, because the boy is to be a Nazirite, set apart to God from birth, and he will begin the deliverance of Israel from the hands of the Philistines."...

Then Manoah prayed to the LORD: "O Lord, I beg you, let the man of God you sent to us come again to teach us how to bring up the boy who is to be born."

God heard Manoah, and the angel of God came again to the woman while she was out in the field; but her husband Manoah was not with her. The woman hurried to tell her husband, "He's here! The man who appeared to me the other day!"

Manoah got up and followed his wife. When he came to the man, he said, "Are you the one who talked to my wife?"

"I am," he said.

So Manoah asked him, "When your words are fulfilled, what is to be the rule for the boy's life and work?"

The angel of the LORD answered, "Your wife must do all that I have told her. She must not eat anything that comes from the grapevine, nor drink any wine or other fermented drink nor eat anything unclean. She must do everything I have commanded her." (Judges 13:2–5, 8–14)

Can you imagine an angel heralding your child's birth? Manoah didn't realize this man was an angel at first, and he invited the guy to dinner. But when the messenger's face appeared in the flame of their sacrifice and ascended upward with the sacred smoke, Manoah and the momma-to-be dove to the dirt in fear and reverence!

The heavenly courier who announced Samson's birth also told his parents to raise him as a Nazirite. And while most Nazirite vows were only made for a season (Paul took Nazirite vows for a short time to praise God for helping him through a difficult period in Corinth; see Acts 18:18), Samson was to be "set apart" for life. The Nazirites were a serious sect among the Jews who consecrated themselves to holiness for God. They showed their dedication to Jehovah by the way they separated themselves from anything remotely "unclean." They scrupulously avoided all grape products—no raisins in their cereal or wine with their spaghetti. They couldn't touch a dead body, and they weren't allowed to cut their hair. It's interesting to note that the Hebrew words used to describe the hair of a Nazirite in Numbers 6:9 and 6:18 are the same words used to describe a high priest's crown in Exodus 29:6 and 39:30. To the Nazirites, their hair was their crowning glory, which somehow brought God glory as well.

When he grew into a man, Samson wasn't very disciplined about the angel's directions for being SET APART. *Instead of following the Nazirite rules, he romanced all the wrong women.*

John the Baptist (whose vows were also for life) is probably the most well-known Nazirite, and he was reputed to be a very hairy man. He dressed in animal skins and had an appetite for bugs and honey. His image emphasizes the fact that Nazirites weren't "normal"; their vows set them apart from everyone else, especially the pagan Philistines who were the archenemies of the Jews.

As a Christian—engaged in the world around you for the sake of the Gospel—are you careful to remain "set apart" from the sin in our culture?

Romeo without a Clue

But when he grew into a man, Samson wasn't very disciplined about the angel's directions for being set apart. Instead of following the Nazirite rules, he romanced all the wrong women. And the first

Philistine girl he married brought him nothing but grief. He told a riddle to some of her buddies at their rehearsal dinner and then bet them thirty new suits that they couldn't figure it out. They couldn't, but they didn't want to lose the bet and be forced to pay the outrageous price of thirty outfits. So they bullied Samson's new wife to betray him and find out the answer to the riddle. She cried the entire seven days of their wedding feast, and Samson finally caved in and coughed up the answer. Which, of course, she immediately shared with the Philistine party guests Samson had stumped. Samson was so mad about their trickery and her deceit that he killed thirty Philistines in a nearby town, gave their clothes to the men who answered his riddle, and left his new bride before the honeymoon began. Later, when his anger had cooled and his passions were hot, Samson went back to his in-laws to reclaim his wife. And things went from bad to worse:

> Later on, at the time of wheat harvest, Samson took a young goat and went to visit his wife. He said, "I'm going to my wife's room." But her father would not let him go in.
>
> "I was so sure you thoroughly hated her," he said, "that I gave her to your friend. Isn't her younger sister more attractive? Take her instead."
>
> Samson said to them, "This time I have a right to get even with the Philistines; I will really harm them." So he went out and caught three hundred foxes and tied them tail to tail in pairs. He then fastened a torch to every pair of tails, lit the torches and let the foxes loose in the standing grain of the Philistines. He burned up the shocks and standing grain, together with the vineyards and olive groves.
>
> When the Philistines asked, "Who did this?" they were told, "Samson, the Timnite's son-in-law, because his wife was given to his friend."
>
> So the Philistines went up and burned her and her father to death. Samson said to them, "Since you've acted like this, I

won't stop until I get my revenge on you." He attacked them viciously and slaughtered many of them. (Judges 15:1–8)

Samson was a one-man Philistine wrecking machine! Not only did he ruin their crops and trash their towns, once he even killed a thousand of them with a donkey jawbone. All to avenge his failed romance with a deceitful woman. After all this, don't you think he'd wise up and marry some nice, quiet Nazirite girl and settle down in the suburbs? Because it's obvious that his poor choice of friends—especially female friends—influenced him to forsake his vows and behave like a bohemian.

Do you have any friends who influence you to forsake your Christian values and behave in ways you know are wrong?

Love Lessons Learned and Lost

Apparently Samson did learn to avoid bad girls for a while; because after the jawbone incident, the Bible says he led Israel for twenty years—with no mention of any additional foxtail fires or bone bashings. Evidently, in an effort to put his rebellious ways behind him, he was careful about whom he was keeping company with.

I met a girl right after college who was in her post-rebellious phase, too. Her name was Jill, and we became fast friends very fast! We worked for the same company, lived in the same apartment complex, liked to play tennis, and loved Jesus. We spent a lot of time together listening to Christian music, reading the Bible, and talking about God. Jill had been raised in a Christian family but rebelled recklessly in high school and college, largely because of her penchant for "bad boys." Since I had a similar prodigal past, we prayed earnestly for each other, especially when one of us had a date! We were committed to helping each other stay on the right path. She was one of my first authentic adult Christian friends, and I was so thankful for her companionship.

We both cried when I packed up my Honda to move to Nashville for a new job. Promising to stay in touch, we hugged tightly and tearfully said goodbye. We talked on the phone a lot right after I left; but soon the busyness of life beat out our best intentions, and we fell out of touch. Still, whenever I thought about Jill, it was always with a prayer and a nostalgic smile.

I guess Jill FORGOT THE COMMITMENT *we made to sexual purity in our twenties; she was back to making the same old mistakes with men.*

Ten years later, I ran into Jill in Durango, Colorado. We'd been living in the same state for several years and didn't know it! I was there with my friend Judy to compete in Durango's world-famous mountain bike race. I was anxious about racing against the women I'd seen strutting around with steely legs and scary tattoos. So I told Judy to park by the Port-o-Potties in case my stomach got as nervous as the rest of my body.

I was standing in line fretting when Jill came out of the bathroom I was waiting for. She looked almost exactly like she did a decade before, and I stepped out of line to greet her. I reached for her arm, grinned broadly, and said, "Hey, Jill, I'm Lisa Harper! From a long time ago in Birmingham!"

Jill looked stunned. I was so excited to see her again and hear how she was doing that I plunged right ahead with our unplanned reunion. But when she politely asked what I was doing for a living and I told her about the ministry I worked with, it was obvious that talking about God made her uncomfortable. Pretty soon her boyfriend—creatively covered in tattoos himself—yelled for her to hurry up and added an expletive to emphasize his wishes. My heart went from delight to disappointment as I watched her walk away.

I tried to talk with her a few more times that day, but Jill didn't seem the least bit interested in renewing our friendship. When one of her friends said something about her living with her boyfriend, she was clearly embarrassed. Later I sent a letter to the address she gave me, but I never heard back from her. I still pray whenever I think of her, but I don't smile anymore.

I guess Jill forgot the commitment we made to sexual purity in our twenties, because it looked like she was back to making the same old mistakes with men. The scripture we memorized about bad company corrupting good character (1 Corinthians 15:33) must've faded in her heart and mind over time. It looked like she had returned to making very bad relational choices—just like Samson did.

Are there any old sin patterns or dangerous relationships that you keep "falling" back into? Why?

The Bible tells us that after twenty years of leading God's people in Israel, Samson fell for another Philistine tart named Delilah. (Delilah lived in the Valley of Sorek—which means *grapes* in Hebrew. You'd think "Grapetown" would be the last place a Nazirite would visit. But Samson, our Romeo without a clue, completely ignored this flashing neon warning sign.) And what a deceitful woman she turned out to be! She tried three times to pry the secret of Samson's strength from him so that her Philistine friends could capture him. Three times he told her a lie. Surely Samson should've woken up from his lust coma when he realized that Delilah shared their pillow talk with his enemies. But he didn't. And after three strikes, she finally got the answer she was looking for:

> Then she said to him, "How can you say, 'I love you,' when you won't confide in me? This is the third time you have made a fool of me and haven't told me the secret of your great strength." With such nagging she prodded him day after day until he was tired to death.
>
> So he told her everything. "No razor has ever been used on my head," he said, "because I have been a Nazirite set apart to God since birth. If my head were shaved, my strength would leave me, and I would become as weak as any other man." (Judges 16:15–17)

When Samson fell asleep—remember, he was "tired to death" from all her nagging—Delilah told the Philistines to shave his head. When he woke up, they overpowered him easily, gouged out his eyes, put him in shackles, and threw him in prison. Poor, dumb Samson! He was betrayed by an immoral woman he shouldn't have been with in the first place. He lost his values, his eyesight, and ultimately his life (although, in God's providence, he died a hero by pulling down pillars at a big Philistine party, killing thousands of pagans). All because he let the wrong people traipse through his heart! Samson's sad story exemplifies what can happen when we don't obey a prodigious proverb: "Above all else, guard your heart, for it is the wellspring of life" (Proverbs 4:23).

Drawbridge Discipline

Henri Nouwen, one of my favorite Christian writers of the last century, gives a modern metaphor to Solomon's proverb in his book

The Inner Voice of Love. In it, Nouwen counsels us to be wary about the people we allow to walk into our lives:

> Think of a medieval castle surrounded by a moat. The drawbridge is the only access to the interior of the castle. The lord of the castle must have the power to decide when to draw the bridge and when to let it down. Without such power, he can become the victim of enemies, strangers, and wanderers. He will never feel at peace in his own castle.
>
> It is important for you to control your own drawbridge. There must be times when you keep your bridge drawn and have the opportunity to be alone or only with those to whom you feel close. Never allow yourself to become public property, where anyone can walk in and out at will.[1]

Just like the verse about guarding our hearts, Nouwen's words about controlling the drawbridge that leads to the interior of our lives is a call to use wisdom in relationships. While Jesus walked this earth, He embraced embezzling tax collectors and sleazy street-walkers, but He never engaged in their sin. He loved them without adopting their lifestyle. And Scripture says we're supposed to look like Jesus. That means that when we lower our drawbridge to let others in, we must not lower our standards like Samson did.

We're called to pursue and perpetuate relationships with the "Philistines" of our culture in order to communicate the compassion and grace of Christ. God's Word literally commands Christians to love non-Christians. However, there's a big difference between befriending an unbeliever for the sake of the Gospel and marrying one.

Like the Nazirites, we need to remember who we're consecrated to, and we need to be careful about the most intimate company we keep. Because pursuing the affections of the wrong people can be very painful. And some of the footprints—and bruises—others

119

leave on our hearts will last a lifetime. The only love relationship that can truly define us without destroying us is God's.

Focusing on His Faithfulness

1. Read the instructions about vows in Psalm 76:11 and Isaiah's prophecy about vows in Isaiah 19:20–21. Then read about the temporary Nazirite vows of Paul and his followers in Acts 18:18 and 21:23. Have you ever made any type of heart "vows" to consecrate yourself to Christ? If so, what did you vow to do or not do? Describe your experience in keeping the vow.

_____

_____

_____

_____

_____

_____

_____

_____

2. Why do you think Samson had such a hard time keeping his Nazirite vows?

_____

_____

_____

_____

_____

_____

_____

3. Have you ever been "tired to death" because of the nagging, consistent temptation of a non-Christian friend or spouse? If so, describe the experience.

_____

_____

_____

_____

_____

_____

_____

4. Do you tend to keep the drawbridge leading to your soul mostly up or down? Why? What changes might you need to make?

_____

_____

_____

_____

_____

_____

5. Who's been making the deepest footprints on your heart lately? In what way?

_____

_____

_____

_____

_____

_____

The mistake is that we have been preaching too much and sympathizing too little.

—Dwight L. Moody

REALLY BIG
ROCKS

One of my favorite—and certainly one of the most familiar—stories in the New Testament is the one about Jesus and the woman who was caught in adultery. I think the reason we've heard so many sermons preached about this story is because it really is an incredible scene to explore. If you're tempted to skip this chapter, thinking that you've already heard everything there is to hear about this woman and her plight, please don't. I'll bet Edison didn't stop pondering electricity just because everyone had a light bulb! Go get a glass of water or a cup of coffee and an apple (or a Twinkie) and settle into a comfortable chair. And read on, trusting God to breathe new life into this tale about the boulder boys and their promiscuous prey.

> But Jesus went to the Mount of Olives. At dawn he appeared again in the temple courts, where all the people gathered around him, and he sat down to teach them. The teachers of the law and the Pharisees brought in a woman caught in adultery. They made her stand before the group and said to Jesus, "Teacher, this woman was caught in the act of adultery. In the

Law Moses commanded us to stone such women. Now what do you say?" They were using this question as a trap, in order to have a basis for accusing him.

But Jesus bent down and started to write on the ground with his finger. When they kept on questioning him, he straightened up and said to them, "If any one of you is without sin, let him be the first to throw a stone at her." Again he stooped down and wrote on the ground.

At this, those who heard began to go away one at a time, the older ones first, until only Jesus was left, with the woman still standing there. Jesus straightened up and asked her, "Woman, where are they? Has no one condemned you?"

"No one, sir," she said.

"Then neither do I condemn you," Jesus declared. "Go now and leave your life of sin." (John 8:1–11)

Just a few hours ago a good friend, Jill Clarke, and I were sitting in my office talking about this poor woman and the punitive men who accused her. Jill is teaching on this passage at a Bible study tomorrow morning, and in anticipation of that, we were discussing how this story epitomizes the Gospel. I summarized it this way: "Broken laws, blame, and disgrace; punishment expected, pardoned by grace." All captured in these eleven verses, sandwiched between accounts of a bunch of Pharisees arguing about the deity of Christ. These probably were the same Pharisees who grabbed this woman from her lover's embrace in order to use her as a pawn in their political war against Jesus. They had memorized the Old Testament Law that allowed for rocks to be thrown at women who committed adultery until the blows killed them. But they knew nothing about the mercy of the Man standing before them in the Temple courts.

Two lessons can be learned from the mistakes these Bible characters made; one is about *hurling* stones, the other is about being *hit* by them. At some time or another, most of us have experienced both.

Check Your Pockets

Hurling stones is a hard habit to break, but it's easy to hide. I'm amazed at how often giant, judgmental stones are slung in Christian settings disguised as prayer requests. The old childhood rhyme "Sticks and stones may break my bones, but words will never hurt me" is a big, fat fable. Verbal stones are perhaps the most damaging of all.

My best friend Kim went through a painful divorce this past year, and rumors swirled around like mosquitoes on a muggy summer night. Partly because she's had some public success in the Christian music arena, people who didn't know the details of her marital situation hurled accusations from the cheap seats. And several of them stomped into the modern temple courts of church leadership demanding her punishment, much like the self-righteous men gripping gravel in the Bible story. I winced at the wounds Kim suffered from other Christians' cutting words. And oh, how I wanted to hurl the biggest brick I could find at their glass houses!

I disagree with most of what the late nineteenth-century philosopher Friedrich Nietzsche taught, because so much of his writing is contrary to Christianity. However, just as God used a jackass for a megaphone to teach Balaam a lesson, I think He spoke through this agnostic man when Nietzsche said, "Whoever fights with

The old childhood rhyme "Sticks and stones may break my bones, but words will never hurt me" is a BIG, FAT FABLE. *Verbal stones are perhaps the most damaging of all.*

monsters should see to it that in the process he does not become a monster." Or to reword it in the context of this chapter, "Whoever recognizes rock throwers had better check his pockets!"

As much as I disliked the self-righteousness of the "religious" people who demanded my friend's head on a platter, I found myself becoming just like them. I struggled with the same type of judgmental spirit I despised in them. There is a big difference between the biblical confrontation described in Matthew 18 or Galatians 6 and the verbal vengeance I was seeking. Retaliating with rocks is never righteous.

What kind of judgmental stones have been burning a hole in your pocket lately?

Deity's Merciful Doodles

Let's stop and think for a minute how the adulteress must've felt when the Pharisees exposed her sin in the Temple court: "The teachers of the law and the Pharisees brought in a woman caught in adultery. They made her stand before the group and said to Jesus, 'Teacher, this woman was caught in the act of adultery'" (John 8:3–4).

The phrase "They made her stand before the group" almost makes me cry. She must've been so embarrassed and ashamed! Remember, the Pharisees "caught" her in the act of adultery, which means she was quite likely nabbed in the nude. And according to many theologians, she was probably set up. Why else was her partner in crime missing? The Law of Moses specifically states in Deuteronomy 22:22 that *both* the man and the woman caught in adultery must die. Did the Pharisees bribe some guy to rat out the woman he was sleeping with? Did she love the Benedict Arnold who betrayed their affair? Had he promised her that he was going to leave his wife and marry her? Did she beg him to throw her something to cover herself with while she was being dragged out of the bedroom? She was probably just as heartbroken as she was humiliated.

And for all this to take place in the Temple court made it even worse. People gathered at the Temple for prayer, to make sacrifices to the Lord, to have their babies blessed, and to worship. It was a busy and crowded place. When the Pharisees came bursting in while Jesus was in the middle of teaching, I bet lots of people who weren't even in His Bible study came running to see what all the commotion was about. Because it wasn't every day that an adulterous woman wrapped in a sheet stood in the middle of the Temple court surrounded by fuming Pharisees. It was like a scene right out of a tawdry Palestinian paperback! And it sure looked like the girl was going to get it.

But when the Pharisees haughtily bent the Law of the Lord for their own agenda, they conveniently forgot what the rest of the Old Testament says about judgment. King David, who was lionized by these same Jewish leaders, said, "Let the LORD judge the peoples" (Psalm 7:8). And the Messiah they thought they'd trapped had spoken these words not long before from a hill on the shore of Galilee:

> Do not judge, or you too will be judged. For in the same way you judge others, you will be judged, and with the measure you use, it will be measured to you.
>
> Why do you look at the speck of sawdust in your brother's eye and pay no attention to the plank in your own eye? How can you say to your brother, "Let me take the speck out of your eye," when all the time there is a plank in your own eye? You

hypocrite, first take the plank out of your own eye, and then you will see clearly to remove the speck from your brother's eye. (Matthew 7:1–5)

If the Pharisees were looking for a sympathetic ear for their self-righteous accusations, they weren't going to find it on His holy head. Jesus—the only One worthy to judge the woman's sinful behavior and pronounce the guilty verdict—was more concerned about her future than her past. So He squatted in the dirt. And the same finger that wrote the Book of the Law these men were trying to kill her with was the finger that doodled in the dust.

With just one statement, Jesus had peeled back the scales COVERING THEIR EYES so they could finally see their own flaws. Even if just for a moment.

Scripture doesn't tell us what Jesus wrote on the ground. But our Messiah bent down to write *something*. Maybe He wrote a list of the accusers' sins. Things they'd done in secret that also carried the sentence of stoning. Or maybe He wrote a scripture about His Father's mercy. Whatever He wrote, it probably distracted the crowd for a minute or two. And I wonder if that's why He bent down—to give the accused woman just a moment of privacy while all eyes peered at the ground to read His inscription.

Then He stood up and said the sentence that silenced everyone: "If any one of you is without sin, let him be the first to throw a stone at her" (John 8:7). And He bent down and started writing again.

The spiritual leaders who until that moment had been holding their ammunition in clenched fists were speechless. They slowly realized their rocks would never touch the imperfect woman in the middle of their condemning circle. Because with just one statement, Jesus had peeled back the scales covering their eyes so they could finally see their own flaws. Even if just for a moment. They had nothing to say that could refute His amazing act of redemption. So they walked away, one at a time, until only the adulterous woman was left standing.

Have you ever found yourself in the middle of a "circle of condemnation"? If so, how did it make you feel?

The Thud of Grace

A good friend of mine, Nicole Johnson, is an actress and author, and she's currently working with the Women of Faith ministry. She travels all over the country helping women understand more about Jesus through her moving monologues during the ministry's conference programs. I went to see her recently when Women of Faith came to Nashville and was blown away by her performance. Her monologue dramatized this story about stones. The following is an excerpt from the words she spoke, now written in a book appropriately titled *Dropping Your Rock*:

> Our rocks will never change the world, only pockmark it with hate and fear. Throwing rocks will never make us more loving. As we clutch and throw our rocks, we reveal our pettiness and our inability to change our own lives. Only when we drop our rocks and choose to love do we become more loving.
>
> So the next time someone trembles in fear and tells you something you really didn't want to know, or you see your sin in someone else's life, or your loved one is braced to feel your stone cold words, you'll know what to do. Loosen your grip, and listen for the flat thud of grace as you choose love over judgment.[1]

The entire time Nicole was sharing this beautiful message on forgiveness, she was walking around the stage carrying a rock. A really big rock. She's petite, and the baby boulder she was waving around was almost as big as her head! By the time the last words rolled off her tongue, tears were streaming down thousands of faces. Then, just before she walked off the stage, she did something very simple, yet so profound: She dropped her rock. It landed on the platform with a loud thud. You could've heard a pin drop in that huge arena. I think most of us were mentally pulling the stones out of our pockets and letting them fall to the floor.

I had to go by my friend Kim's house tonight to borrow her copy of Nicole's book because I've loaned mine out. And I couldn't help but notice how Nicole had inscribed it; I smiled at how kind and empathetic her words were. She knows exactly how Kim felt when the biggest rocks found their mark, because she recently walked through a painful divorce herself. I don't remember exactly how that old Indian proverb goes—something like "Don't judge someone else until you've walked a mile in her moccasins"—but it's still very sage advice.

Which is more evident in your life: compassion or a critical spirit?

Bullies with Bruises

The second lesson from this gem in John's Gospel has to do with being hit by stones. Or more specifically, with the tendency for people who've been hit by stones to turn into hurlers themselves. Because I think Nicole's grace toward Kim is rare. I think most people who've been pockmarked by the self-righteous stones of others are the same ones who hurl back the hardest. Even our justice system will tell you that almost all abusers were at one time abused themselves. Big men who are in jail for beating their wives typically started out as little boys with welts. Underneath the jagged exterior of a judgmental person is usually a wounded heart that's never really been healed.

I wonder what would've happened to the woman caught in adultery if she hadn't run into Jesus. What if her accusers hadn't been convicted of their own sin and slunk away that day? What if their rocks had found their mark? If she had survived their beating, do you think she would've been grateful for the way they'd punished her? Or do you think she would've picked up a few rocks for herself and tucked them away for safekeeping, knowing that one day the time would come when she could hurl them?

Jesus wasn't merely the righteous judge in this story whose wise **COMPASSION** *caused the Pharisees to leave the adulteress alone. He was also the healer of her broken and battered soul.*

A few years ago I met a woman who became one of my harshest critics. She said a lot of ugly things about me personally and professionally. Although she smiled to my face, she threw some pretty pointy rocks behind my back. And when I finally confronted her, she wrote a scathing letter attacking my integrity and sent it to several people I respected and worked with. I was angry and perplexed, wondering what I'd done to offend her so thoroughly. I wasn't sure why she thought I was pond scum, but I sure wanted her to quit hurling insults as hard as she could.

I found out later that this woman had been abused and belittled for years. And she'd become so bitter and insecure by the time our paths crossed that she'd built up quite an impressive rock collection. Our insignificant personality conflict triggered a significant avalanche that had been poised to fall for a long, long time. Some of the rocks she hit me with were so old they had diamonds in the middle of them!

Jesus wasn't merely the righteous judge in this story whose wise compassion caused the Pharisees to leave the adulteress alone. He was also the healer of her broken and battered soul. Because while the men's tangible rocks never touched her skin, their evil entrapment and barbed hostility had sliced her to the bone.

By the grace of God, however, this abused woman didn't become a statistic. She didn't start stockpiling stones. Her wounded heart didn't have time to fester and scab over with hardness. Before it could, Jesus lanced it with His mercy.

"Woman, where are they? Has no one condemned you?" He asked her. And when she answered, "No one, sir," He told her, "Then neither do I condemn you" (John 8:10–11).

Isn't it a miracle that the only One worthy of condemning us chooses to pardon us with redemptive compassion? Isn't His relentless love amazing? When we have rocks bulging in our pockets, we need to ask the Holy Spirit to pry off the planks covering our eyes. Not just so we can see our own sin, but also so we'll notice the pockmarks we haven't yet asked God to heal. Because those of us who've been hit by self-righteous rocks can choose not to hurl them back. And once we allow Jesus to bandage our bruises, we won't even want to throw stones anymore.

Focusing on His Faithfulness

1. What words spoken about you in the past have hurt you the most? Why?

_____

_____

_____

_____

_____

_____

2. Have you ever wanted to hurl a big brick at the reputation of one of your accusers? Did you? What happened?

_____

_____

_____

_____

_____

_____

3. Read 2 Samuel 16:5–14. It's a really interesting story about a guy who literally pelted King David with rocks! Then turn to 2 Samuel 19:14–23 for the rest of the story. What do you think about David's response to Shimei the stone thrower?

_____

_____

_____

_____

_____

_____

4. Do you agree or disagree with the statement that "Christians are the only ones who shoot their wounded"? Why?

_____

_____

_____

_____

_____

_____

5. What emotional bruises caused by the caustic criticism of others still hurt you when they're poked? Spend some time alone in prayer asking Jesus to heal those bruises.

_____

_____

_____

_____

_____

_____

_____

_____

_____

The world dwarfs us all, but God dwarfs the world. The world is his footstool, above which he sits secure. He is greater than the world and all that is in it, so that all the feverish activity of its bustling millions does no more to affect him than the chirping and jumping of grasshoppers in the summer sun does to affect us.

—J. I. Packer

MISUNDERSTANDING MAJESTY

A friend of mine, Paige Benton (who also happens to be one of the best Bible teachers I've ever had the privilege to sit under—she teaches at Park Cities Presbyterian in Dallas, and she's worth the drive if you're within a few hundred miles!), tells the story of a bright little boy in a kindergarten Sunday school class. It was the Sunday before Easter, and the Sunday school teacher wanted to remind the children of what Easter was really all about. So she started by asking the class a question that would help them understand that many of the holidays we celebrate center around Jesus.

"Who can tell me the meaning of Christmas?" she asked.

One of the little six-year-old boys raised his hand and said, "It's when Jesus became incarnate, and all the angels sang, and the shepherds worshiped, and the wise men came."

"That was an excellent answer, Billy," the teacher said, thinking, *Boy, his parents must be teachers or something.* Then she asked, "Now, who can tell us the meaning of today, Palm Sunday?"

The same little boy raised his hand and answered, "It's when

Jesus entered Jerusalem as the Messiah, and all the people laid down palm branches, and it was the beginning of the last week of His life."

The teacher grinned at Billy's enthusiastic response and continued her line of questioning. "Can anyone else explain what happened on Good Friday?"

The rest of the little boys and girls were quiet and wide-eyed, unsure of the answer. After waiting for someone else to speak up, the teacher nodded at young Einstein, and he answered again: "That's when Jesus was crucified on a cross for our sins, and the temple curtain was torn in two, and He gave up His spirit to the Father."

Impressed and bemused, the teacher smiled at Billy and said, "Why don't you go ahead and tell us about Easter?"

Billy straightened his shoulders, cleared his throat, and proudly proclaimed, "That's when Jesus came out of the tomb, but then He saw His shadow, so He went back in for another three weeks!"

Although we probably wouldn't confuse the resurrection of God Incarnate with Groundhog Day, most of us are still a lot like that little boy! We might know a lot about God, but like that precocious six-year-old, we're immature in our understanding of who He really is. We tend to concentrate on just a few facets of His infinite character. And we enthusiastically memorize verses and read books that only highlight our particular point of interest, essentially paring God down to a one-dimensional deity.

The word for this belittling behavior is *anthropomorphic*. It's a mouthful of syllables that Webster's defines as "ascribing human form or attributes to a being or thing not human, especially to a deity." Which basically means trying to define or describe God with human words or terms within the sphere of human experience. It's impossible! We can't begin to describe the Creator of the Universe with our dinky adjectives! Even the most brilliant theologians throughout history have never come up with an explanation that describes His awesomeness. He is way beyond the wordiest description of the most profound writers.

Simply put, His infinite majesty is more than our finite minds can comprehend. So we compensate by creating mental caricatures of God and then living our lives in relation to the cartoon deity in our head. But comfortable, comprehensible images of God are dangerous, because they can't command the reverence and respect due to the King of Kings and Lord of Lords. I think one of the biggest barriers to living a godly life—defined by repentance and humility—is this tendency to see God as "too small."

Big Daddy

My real dad isn't a very big man. He's about five-foot-eight and 160 pounds or so—definitely not imposing or intimidating size-wise. But I'll never forget the day he grew about ten feet tall in my eyes. My cousin and constant childhood companion, Brenda, and I were riding with Dad in his truck. We were both about twelve, still happy to ride along on extended errand runs (especially since Dad always bought us Cokes and candy!). I don't remember where we were going, but I can remember the exact intersection where the incident happened. We were stopped at the light, and a teenager recklessly raced his car beside to us and began screaming at us. Evidently he thought Dad had cut him off when he changed lanes. The teenager yelled his displeasure with foul language and punctuated his points with obscene gestures.

Before we knew it, Dad had jumped out of the truck and had Mr.

Profanity cowering in his car. Dad lectured him loudly for "cussing in front of my kids!" And he didn't let up when the light changed, either. By the time Dad let him go, the juvenile delinquent had promised never to use that type of language in front of young ladies again!

Brenda and I were glued to our seats the whole time, watching Dad with wide-eyed wonder. We'd never had our honor defended publicly before. When Dad got back in the truck and put his arm around us before pulling away, I was so glad he was *my daddy*. My heart swelled with pride and respect, and I couldn't help grinning. Dad seemed bigger to me somehow.

Do you think of your biological father as a "big" man? Why or why not?

Just as my adolescent eyes opened up to more of my dad's character, we need to open our spiritual eyes to more of God's character. We are called to worship and revere all that He is instead of just those facets of Him that we find favorable. We need to start seeing God "bigger." Because a myopic misunderstanding of Him leads to lackluster worship and halfhearted obedience.

We need to open our spiritual eyes to more of God's character. We are called to WORSHIP AND REVERE *all that He is instead of just those facets of Him that we find favorable.*

Like most evangelicals, my favorite facets of God are those on His "soft side." I delight in the sermons, books, and Bible studies that focus on the grace and mercy of God. I love the mental picture of Him as our Rescuer and our Redeemer. One of my favorite passages in the New Testament is in Romans 8, where Paul writes that the Holy

Spirit gives us the right to call God *Abba*, meaning "Daddy." The biblical concept of God as a loving Father—who listens to us, beckons us to climb up on His lap, and embraces us—makes me feel secure and comfortable.

Yet Scripture talks about *fearing* God more times than it does *loving* Him. God is much more than a doting, heavenly "Daddy." He is also a consuming fire, so altogether holy and fearsome that we would likely be paralyzed in His presence.

Opening Anthropomorphic Eyes

The Bible says that after Moses attended the Ten Commandment Conference with the Creator of the Universe, his face was so shiny that it scared everybody half to death:

> When Moses came down from Mount Sinai with the two tablets of the Testimony in his hands, he was not aware that his face was radiant because he had spoken with the LORD. When Aaron and all the Israelites saw Moses, his face was radiant, and they were afraid to come near him. (Exodus 34:29–30)

God's majesty was so powerful on that mountaintop that the mere leftover reflection on Moses' face was enough to freeze the Israelites in fear. In fact, Moses had to start wearing a bag over his head (Scripture actually calls it a "veil") after spending time in God's presence so that his countenance wouldn't cause temporary blindness!

Think about it: The same God who runs toward prodigals and hugs them is so awesome that His residual radiance is like the brightest morning sunrise. We put decals on our cars that call Him a "copilot," but the truth is we would tremble in terror if we even glimpsed His reflection. His power and glory call for bended knees and bowed hearts, not trite bumper-sticker theology.

When I was in a sorority in college, my best friend at the time, Tammy, was in charge of the "discipline committee." So when Tammy told me that she needed to talk with me about an incident at a fraternity party, I wasn't very nervous. I walked into the sorority chapter room at our appointed meeting time and smiled as I faced my very serious-looking friend. We were alone in the room, and I got a little tickled during the awkward silence. But then Tammy proceeded to give me a stern lecture on inappropriate behavior (I had kissed my boyfriend on the dance floor) for a Kappa Delta "lady."

I fidgeted and giggled while she chastised me, surprised by her angry response. She was absolutely furious with my flippancy. I thought, *Gosh, it's not that big of a deal. I don't know what all the fuss is about!* In my immaturity I had minimized Tammy's position and her responsibility to help instill discipline among unruly Kappa Deltas. I took her authority far too lightly.

I'm certainly not equating God's holiness with sorority protocol, but we tend to take His position and authority far too lightly as well. We see the "hard side" of God through anthropomorphic eyes and think that His righteous anger, discipline, and wrath are incongruent with the God of love, patience, and mercy we sing about. If we could peer into each other's hearts and minds, we'd probably find out that most of us simply don't understand those "harder" facets of God's nature.

What facets of God's character are the most confusing to you?

Doubting Divine Discipline

If it makes you feel any better, King David, whom Scripture refers to as "a man after God's own heart," also had a hard time understanding God's divine discipline. The story begins with David requesting that the ark of the covenant be brought back to Israel:

> David conferred with each of his officers, the commanders of thousands and commanders of hundreds. He then said to the whole assembly of Israel, "If it seems good to you and if it is the will of the LORD our God, let us send word far and wide to the rest of our brothers throughout the territories of Israel, and also to the priests and Levites who are with them in their towns and pasturelands, to come and join us. Let us bring the ark of our God back to us, for we did not inquire of it during the reign of Saul." The whole assembly agreed to do this, because it seemed right to all the people. (1 Chronicles 13:1–4)

Do you remember what the ark of the covenant was? Some people get it confused with the boat that Noah and all the animals floated around on. Others immediately think of the Indiana Jones movie. But this biblical box is a little different! The Israelites built the ark of the covenant after they escaped from Egypt, fashioning it according to the directions God gave Moses on top of Mount Sinai (when Moses got the case of shimmering skin!). It was a very ornate box—*ark* is a Hebrew word that basically means "box"—made out of acacia wood that was overlaid with pure gold inside and out. It was almost four feet long and a little more than two feet high, with gold molding all around it. There were gold rings on each of the four feet of the ark so that acacia wood poles (also covered in gold) could be inserted in the rings in order to carry it. The top of the ark was called the "atonement cover"; it, too, was covered in pure gold, with two cherubim

If it makes you feel any better, King David, whom Scripture refers to as "a man after God's own heart," also had a hard time UNDERSTANDING *God's divine discipline.*

mounted on each end. Inside the ark were the stone tablets that God inscribed on the mountain with Moses, along with Aaron's "budding" staff and a jar of manna.

The ark of the covenant and its contents were proof of God's presence with the Israelites. They carried it with them to the Promised Land and even carried it with them when they marched into battle. It was a sacred symbol of God's favor and power—the most holy and revered treasure of the Jewish people. So for David to give instructions for the ark to be brought back to Jerusalem was a really big deal. And the people threw a really big party to celebrate. The Bible says: "They moved the ark of God from Abinadab's house on a new cart, with Uzzah and Ahio guiding it. David and all the Israelites were celebrating with all their might before God, with songs and harps, lyres, tambourines, cymbals and trumpets" (1 Chronicles 13:7–8).

But even though they were celebrating with all their might, the party pooped out when they arrived at Kidon because

> Uzzah reached out his hand to steady the ark, because the oxen had stumbled. The Lord's anger burned against Uzzah, and he struck him down because he had put his hand on the ark. So he died there before God. Then David was angry because the Lord's wrath had broken out against Uzzah, and to this day that place is called Perez Uzzah. (1 Chronicles 13:9–11)

Perez Uzzah means "outbreak against Uzzah," and "outbreak" is an understatement. "Dead in his tracks" is more like it! David was dumbfounded. He couldn't believe what had just happened. There he was, leading a grand parade celebrating the ark's return to Jerusalem, and God had to go and spoil everything by zapping some poor guy who was just trying to do his job. Or so it seemed.

Remember, at this point in his life David had been following God faithfully for many years. He was not some young guy who just met God at youth camp. He had trusted God when he faced Goliath before he even started shaving; he had refused to kill King Saul when he had the chance, because he knew he wasn't supposed to harm God's anointed (even if God's anointed had become a jealous murderer); and he had spent years on the run, hiding out in caves because he trusted God's sovereign timetable over his own career plans. When he finally became king, he'd led the Israelites to unprecedented victory and favor in the name of the Lord. No, he didn't doubt God's authority; he'd seen Him turn giants into Jell-O and caves into cathedrals. But he just couldn't understand why God would kill Uzzah. It seemed unduly harsh—and David got mad.

When was the last time you got mad at God because you didn't understand Him?

Justified Justice

I can understand why David was bugged. At first glance it does seem as if Uzzah should have been a hero instead of a goat. According to the story, while the Israelites were moving the ark back to a place of prominence in Israel, Uzzah instinctively put out his hand to steady the ark and keep it from falling on the ground when the ox—clumsy as oxen can be—stumbled. To be killed for caring about the safety and security of the ark of the covenant does seem pretty punitive. Do you think maybe God was having a bad day, and He took it out on poor, innocent Uzzah?

Of course not! Uzzah wasn't just some guy off the street pitching in to help in the ark parade. Uzzah was a Levite, born into the tribe chosen to work in the Temple. (Prior to the construction of Solomon's temple, God's temple was actually a tent called the "Tent of Meeting.") Not only that, but Uzzah's family was the clan of Kohathites, who were given the honor and responsibility of caring for the holy things consecrated to God in the Tent of Meeting.

There's a whole chapter in the Book of Numbers that specifies exactly how Uzzah and his relatives were supposed to take care of the articles used for ministering in the sanctuary. And the most explicit and serious directions involved the ark of the covenant. As a little boy in "Ark Academy," Uzzah spent years taking classes like "Packing Sanctified Stuff 101" and "No Peeking or You'll Be Pulverized." He memorized every mandate from God regarding the ark and the other religious articles in his keeping. He knew exactly what he was allowed to do and what he wasn't allowed to do. And one of God's decrees said that no Kohathite could look at the ark of the covenant—much less touch it—under any circumstances.

What God does is always CONSISTENT *with who He is. And who God is, is perfect.*

So when Uzzah reached out and steadied the ark with his hand, he was defying the Law of God, which he knew like the back of his hand. He was minimizing God's absolute authority, arrogantly thinking that his touch on the ark was better than the ark touching the ground. Plus, he shouldn't have been transporting the ark on an ox cart in the first place! According to God's Law, the ark was supposed to be carried with acacia poles; that's why it had rings on the corners. But Uzzah chose convenience over obedience. His sin was not an innocuous, petty slip; it was a flagrant foul—and he died as a result.

God doesn't sound like a benevolent copilot in this story, does He? And that's hard for most of us grace-centered evangelicals to swallow. Like David, we can't quite comprehend how the wrath of God is congruent with His never-ending mercy. His "soft side" and His "hard side" seem diametrically opposed.

But they aren't. Because what God does is always consistent with who He is. And who God is, is *perfect*. It's His divine nature to be holy and righteous. To be capricious or unduly harsh would be in opposition to righteousness and thus to God's character. He can't respond in any way that transgresses His own holiness. So He wasn't "out of line" or unjust when He killed Uzzah. He was simply acting as a sovereign, omnipotent Ruler who expects His children to obey Him. He will always be warranted in His wrath and justified in His justice.

God doesn't fit the one-dimensional cartoon deities floating around in our heads. And some facets of His character will probably always make us a little uncomfortable. But that doesn't make Him any less perfect. My favorite explanation of God's complex character is in C. S. Lewis's well-loved series *The Chronicles of Narnia*. Narnia is a make-believe land full of talking animals, good and evil, and a great lion king named Aslan. When the human children in the story— Susan, Lucy, and Edmund—ask Mr. and Mrs. Beaver about Aslan (whom they haven't met yet), Lewis writes a wonderful, analogous description of God:

> "Is—is he a man?" asked Lucy. "Aslan a man!" said Mr. Beaver sternly. "Certainly not. I tell you he is the King of the wood and the son of the great Emperor-beyond-the-Sea. Don't you know who is the King of Beasts? Aslan is a lion—the Lion, the great Lion."
> "Ooh!" said Susan, "I'd thought he was a man. Is he—quite safe? I shall feel rather nervous about meeting a lion."

"That you will, dearie, and no mistake," said Mrs. Beaver; "if there's anyone who can appear before Aslan without their knees knocking, they're either braver than most or else just silly."

"Then he isn't safe?" said Lucy.

"Safe?" said Mr. Beaver; "don't you hear what Mrs. Beaver tells you? Who said anything about safe? 'Course he isn't safe. But he's good. He's the king, I tell you."[1]

God isn't our copilot or our buddy or some kind of safe Santa Claus. He's bigger than that. He is the King of Kings—I tell you!—more powerful and wonderful than even the widest human eyes can see or imagine!

Focusing on His Faithfulness

1. What are some of the anthropomorphic phrases you've heard people use to describe God (e.g., "copilot," "the man upstairs," etc.)?

_____

_____

_____

_____

_____

_____

2. List some of your favorite facets of God's character.

_____

_____

_____

_____

_____

_____

3. What was your initial reaction to the wrath Uzzah received?

_____

_____

_____

_____

_____

_____

_____

4. Have you ever wondered about the "fairness" of the wrath of God? Do you have a different perspective now? How so?

_____

_____

_____

_____

_____

_____

5. Does your perception of God lean more toward His "hard side" or His "soft side"? Explain.

_____

_____

_____

_____

_____

_____

6. Write out a prayer asking God to open the eyes of your heart so that you can "see Him bigger."

_____

_____

_____

_____

_____

_____

_____

_____

_____

What makes us hesitate and stumble? It is fear, I think, that makes one cling nostalgically to the last moment or clutch greedily toward the next.... But how to exorcise it? It can only be exorcised by its opposite, love.

—Anne Morrow Lindbergh

chapter
eleven

BALKING BEHIND
BARRIERS

A few months ago my friend Kim was driving her two boys, Graham and Benjamin, home from school. She was tooling along, humming absentmindedly with the radio, when she overheard Graham (who's eight) exclaim to Benji (who's four), "Wow, look at those hooters!"

Quickly panning the neighborhood, Kim noticed a woman leaning over in her garden and assumed that Graham's crass comment to his baby brother was in reference to the woman's conspicuous cleavage. She sharply instructed the boys to stop talking until they got home. Then the thought came to her: *I wonder where Graham heard that? I thought he wouldn't learn words like that yet, especially since he's in a Christian school!*

She pulled into their driveway still pondering how to reprimand such rude behavior. When the car came to a stop, she turned to face her quiet children and launched into a lecture about the importance of treating all women with respect. She went on to emphasize how boys should never, ever use slang or off-color words to describe the female body, which God had created. And she closed by saying that she never, ever wanted to hear *hooter* come out of either of their mouths again!

That's when a puzzled Graham piped up and asked Kim what a "hooter" was. As she soon discovered, his comment to Benjamin had to do with the new *scooters* they saw in one of the yards they drove past, not female anatomy! That misunderstanding of one little word caused a whole lot of trouble—accidentally popping open a Pandora's box she had hoped would stay closed until her boys hit puberty!

Misinterpreting Intimacy

The Song of Songs has also caused a whole lot of trouble through the centuries whenever people have lifted the lid on this box of biblical poetry. Jeanne Guyon, an emotive Christian woman living in France in the seventeenth century, dared to study and write a commentary on this little book in the middle of the Bible. And she was audacious enough to make the book personal, using it to illustrate the love relationship between Christ and Christians. In a culture of rigid religious tradition and piety, she bravely asserted that it was possible for believers to have a deeper union with God—one that could be thought of in the terms of "spiritual marriage." She wrote that the "kiss of His mouth" illustration in the Song of Songs is nothing less than the vital communication of the Word of God to us.

Her belief that we could have a passionate love relationship with our Redeemer made some of the most powerful churchmen in Europe—including the Archbishop of France—very angry. And of course most of the important toes she stepped on had taken the vow of celibacy, so the erotic poetry found in this Old Testament book was already way out of their comfort zone! A committee of spiritual and political hot shots was formed to investigate Madame Guyon's writings. And after reading her colorful commentary, they sent her to prison for her "blasphemy."

You know, that's what got Jesus in trouble with the religious leaders of His day, too. Teaching that we could actually have a love relationship with our heavenly Father.

While the eight chapters that Solomon probably penned have been misunderstood more than any other passages of Scripture (except perhaps those in Revelation), they paint the most beautiful picture of the intimacy we can have with our Savior. This lavish love poem—while admittedly difficult to interpret—is well worth wading into. And like the other passages we've looked at so far in this book, the Song of Songs has a character—a newlywed named Beloved—whose bumbling mistakes we can identify with and learn from.

One of Beloved's biggest blunders is found in the middle of chapter 2:

> Listen! My lover! Look! Here he comes, leaping across the mountains, bounding over the hills. My lover is like a gazelle or a young stag. Look! There he stands behind our wall, gazing through the windows, peering through the lattice. My lover spoke and said to me, "Arise, my darling, my beautiful one, and come with me. See! The winter is past; the rains are over and gone. Flowers appear on the earth; the season of singing has come, the cooing of doves is heard in our land. The fig tree forms its early fruit; the blossoming vines spread their fragrance. Arise, come, my darling; my beautiful one, come with me." (Song of Songs 2:8–13)

We're going to look at these verses using a *christological* approach—which means we're going to look at them through the same glasses that got Jeanne Guyon thrown in the slammer! For the sake of application, we'll look at the "Lover" in these scriptures as a metaphor illustrating the Lord. And we'll look at "Beloved," the narrative voice that describes her Lover as a gazelle, as a metaphor for Christians.

Everything starts out great in verse eight with Beloved describing her Lover as one who was "leaping across the mountains" and "bounding over the hills" to get to her. This "godly guy" was determined to jump over every hurdle standing between Him and His Beloved! This description of the Lover's devotion is so good that Diana Ross and the Supremes borrowed it for one of their most famous lyrics: "Ain't no mountain high enough…"!

Have you ever thought about God as a "pursuing" God? What hurdles did He leap over to capture your heart?

Like me, you've probably heard people say that God is a gentleman who knocks at the door of our heart but won't come in uninvited. I don't like that analogy. In fact, I think the scripture people refer to (Revelation 3:20) is taken out of context, because their interpretation paints a picture of our omnipotent, omniscient, majestic God—who holds lightning in His fist—standing outside a door like a shy schoolboy selling candy bars for band camp. If God is such a timid gentleman, twisting His hat in His hands outside our heart's door, then what in the world happened to Paul on the Damascus Road? Did God just forget His manners when He blinded him? He didn't *stand outside the door* of Paul's heart—He blew it off its hinges!

I think if we look at the entire context of Scripture, we will find that God pursues us with an irresistible grace. Like the Lover in Solomon's Song of Songs, He will overcome any obstacle that stands between Him and His beloved.

But where was Beloved (illustrating those of us who are Christians) while her Lover (illustrating our Savior) was jumping over every obstacle to be with her? Instead of rushing to embrace her gallant Husband, she was waiting behind a wall (which she misrepresented as "our wall")! Beloved immaturely assumed that standing behind a wall was a good thing. And hiding behind hedges is a mistake many of us repeat, especially once we've made a commitment to Christ.

According to the first chapter of the Song of Songs, Beloved had experienced intimacy with her Lover before she started crouching behind barriers: "Let him kiss me with the kisses of his mouth—for your love is more delightful than wine" (Song of Songs 1:2). In modern terminology we'd say that she had checked a commitment card, or walked an aisle, or made some type of profession of faith. Then she probably got sprinkled or dunked and signed up for a Bible study. She experienced the first sweet throes of salvation in chapter 1. Now she wanted everything to stay just as it was.

Take a few minutes to remember the day or the season of your salvation. How much have you grown spiritually since then—not in head knowledge, but in trust and hope and obedience?

Secure Superficiality

Like Peter on the Mount of Transfiguration, many of us would like to stay on the first mountaintop of spiritual intimacy. We have saving faith in Jesus Christ—so we're not going to burn in hell—and we'd like to keep things just the way they are, thank you. "Abba" sounds pretty good to us, but "Lover" is a little too much. We'd rather skip over the scripture that says that God is not only our *Maker*, but also our *Husband* (Isaiah 54:5). That kind of relationship with God doesn't feel safe at all, because we've grown accustomed to a *lack of intimacy*. We're so used to being misunderstood, ignored, and manipulated that superficial relationships have become the norm in our lives. Superficial attention and affection have become much more comfortable than a deep love affair with a heavenly "Husband."

Consequently, we'd much rather stay safe behind our walls than risk being completely known by God. His relentless love makes many of us uncomfortable. And our souls suffer as a result.

John Eldredge, one of my favorite *living* Christian writers, talks about the spiritual crisis of our shriveled souls in his book *The Journey of Desire*:

> Christianity has come to the point where we believe that there is no higher aspiration for the human soul than to be nice. We are producing a generation of men and women whose greatest virtue is that they don't offend anyone. Then we wonder why there is not more passion for Christ. How can we hunger and thirst for righteousness if we have ceased hungering and thirsting altogether? As C. S. Lewis said, "We castrate the gelding and bid him be fruitful."[1]

When we hide behind carefully constructed religious walls like Beloved, we emasculate hope. "Wall women" temper their expectations and settle for so much less than the abundant life God promises us. Behind barriers, we don't sense the nearness of His presence or hear the songs Zephaniah says He sings over us. It's like the difference between standing outside of Starbucks with your nose pressed to the window and walking into the store, inhaling the aroma of fresh brewed coffee, and savoring a cup. God wants us to come out from behind our walls and really *be with Him:* "My lover spoke and said to me, 'Arise, my darling, my beautiful one, and come with me'" (Song of Songs 2:10).

An acquaintance of mine is obviously having a hard time letting her youngest child grow up. Although the boy is already in school, she still dresses him in fancy, hand-smocked white jumpers (which I think are cute on babies and toddlers, but not especially cute on elementary students). And while the other classmates roughhouse on the playground, he sits by himself and pines away for his pacifier. I think someone should summon the courage to tell his momma that he's too old to be dressed like a baby and beg for his "binky."

Solomon's poetry is a pointed message telling Christians that we're too old to behave like spiritual babies and camp out behind fences full of fear. We need to grow up and let loose our longing for deeper intimacy with God.

The Tenderness of Tumbling Walls

The issue of deeper intimacy with God used to scare my friend Kelly, who is an extremely poised, elegant woman. She and her semi-retired husband live in a beautiful beach home with a yacht in the backyard and manicured walls that were erected to keep others on the outside. When I first met her, there were also metaphorical walls around Kelly's heart that kept others on the outside and painful secrets on the inside. Secrets Kelly kept well-hidden for a very long time.

You see, Kelly was sexually abused by her father throughout her childhood. She married at fifteen, mostly to get away from him. She never told anyone about the abuse except her husband. But several years ago she decided she should tell her only daughter, Julie, because she wanted Julie to be careful when the grandchildren visited their great-grandfather.

After Kelly painfully poured out the story to her daughter, Julie told her mother that she didn't need to worry about the grandkids. Julie already knew that she could never leave the children alone with their great-grandfather, because he had abused her, too. Kelly was devastated, as you can imagine. She hadn't been able to protect her own precious child!

Less than a year later, Kelly's father was dying, and she and Julie were the only ones left in the family who were able to care for him. In spite of the horrific wounds they suffered because of his wretched sin, they both chose to extend mercy. They spent several hours a day in his hospital room, feeding him and trying to make him as comfortable as possible. He rallied for a "deathbed confession" and asked the two women to forgive him for what he did to them. Then he died a few days later.

Kelly told me that she didn't know whether to grieve or rejoice when he finally died. She drove home from the hospital in a daze and walked from the garage through the laundry room, absentmindedly flipping the pages of the prayer calendar she kept there to that day's date. Glancing down, she saw that the scripture inscribed on the calendar for that date—the day her very unsafe earthly father died—was this: "See! The winter is past; the rains are over and gone. Flowers appear on the earth; the season of singing has come" (Song of Songs 2:11–12).

When she read those verses, elegant, poised Kelly slid to the floor and sobbed. She had worked so hard for more than forty years to stay safe behind her walls, because the alternative was too frightening. She knew Jesus as her Redeemer and Savior—but she hadn't experienced Him as her Refuge. She hadn't allowed herself to feel the sweet embrace of the Lover of her troubled soul. She had shied away from the fact that her merciful Maker was also a Husband—who promises to be close to His brokenhearted beloved. Now the wall that separated Kelly from a truly intimate relationship with God came tumbling down. And her season of singing started in a sanctuary full of Tide.

Watchman Nee, a wonderful theologian and author from the mid-twentieth century, says in his commentary on the Song of Songs that the "rain" in verse eleven symbolizes *winter* rain—the kind of rain that chills us to the bone and makes us want to stay safe inside, curled up by the fire with a good book and a cup of cocoa. Nee goes on to explain that these two verses (which the Lover spoke lovingly to Beloved, and which God whispered lovingly to Kelly) refer to our position as a result of the Cross. Because, he says, whenever spring is mentioned *after* winter in Scripture, it illustrates the Crucifixion and the Resurrection. It symbolizes the hope we have, because Jesus took the worst of winter with Him on Calvary's tree. As His beloved bride, we can come out from behind our walls of self-protection because of the promise of Easter.

Beloved finally did. Although she started out as the poster child for Superficiality Anonymous, she wound up being a shining star of spiritual intimacy: "I belong to my lover, and his desire is for me. Come, my lover, let us go to the countryside, let us spend the night in the villages" (Song of Songs 7:10–11).

Beloved grew up. She no longer hid herself behind a wall while her Lover tried to coax her to come away with Him. Instead, she actually initiated an intimate getaway for the two of them. She wanted to go wherever He went, even if it meant leaving home and spending the night in an unfamiliar place. "Come, my lover, let us go...." These aren't the words of a Martha-Stewart wannabe consumed with decorating walls to keep herself in and others out;

they are the words of a missionary-in-the-making, head-over-heels in love with her heavenly Husband—and ready to tell the world all about Him.

Focusing on His Faithfulness

1. How did God pursue you before you committed your life to Him? How does He continue to pursue you?

_____

_____

_____

_____

_____

_____

2. Describe some of the "heart changes" that have taken place in you since becoming a believer.

_____

_____

_____

_____

_____

_____

3. Does the phrase "accustomed to a lack of intimacy" describe you in any way? If so, how?

_____

_____

_____

_____

_____

_____

4. Do the words *Husband* or *Lover* used to describe God in Scripture make you uncomfortable? Is so, why?

_____

_____

_____

_____

_____

_____

_____

_____

5. Write out a prayer asking God to reveal areas where you're uncomfortable with His tender affection and relentless love. You might enjoy reading Jeanne Guyon's or Watchman Nee's commentary on the Song of Songs.

_____

_____

_____

_____

_____

_____

_____

_____

But trust is firm belief, it is faith in full flower.

—E. M. Bounds

THE MARK OF
MATURITY

We've spent the last eleven chapters sifting through the stories of some of the clumsiest characters in the Bible. Donkey beaters, law lovers, grace abusers, rock throwers, and real dumb Romeos. Men and women whose lives were full of foibles—not unlike us. I don't know about you, but I'm ready to read about someone who *did it right*. Someone who was faithful when things didn't go his or her way. Someone who trusted God in the midst of turmoil. Someone like my friend Pammy Markle.

The first time I met Pammy, we were at a formal event celebrating the dedication of Focus on the Family's new headquarters in Colorado Springs. The event was held in a hotel ballroom with about three or four hundred guests; and even though it was crowded, I noticed Pammy right away. Wearing a sparkly blue dress, she was smiling broadly and talking in a sweet southern accent to anyone who glanced her way. If you didn't know any better, you'd think she was running for office! She was so friendly and so pretty that I arrogantly assumed she was probably as shallow as she was shiny. Boy, was I wrong.

Have you ever "judged a book by its cover" and been completely wrong? Have you ever apologized to the "book"?

The Illusion of Perfection

A few weeks later Pammy and I got together for an "official" Focus on the Family women's ministry visit. And since I didn't know Pammy personally, I asked her if she'd tell me her story: where she grew up, how she became a Christian, how she met her husband, etc. She seemed genuinely kind and kept trying to turn the focus of the conversation back toward me. But when I insisted that I really wanted to hear about *her*, she began to tell me about her childhood, her family, and how she met her husband, Eric, on the first day of her freshman year in college. She was standing under an oak tree, and he walked over and introduced himself. They basically fell in love at first sight, and sure enough, they got married two years later. After college Eric joined the Marines to become a jet pilot.

"Yes, Pammy, it looks as if Eric is dead," the commanding officer said. And at THAT MOMENT, *the bottom fell out of Pammy's "perfect" world.*

I was now on my second or third Diet Coke, thinking Pammy's story sounded like a fairy tale! "Handsome military hero falls in love with pretty southern blonde, and they live happily ever after." And as Pammy continued her story, it did seem like she and Eric were going to live happily ever after. They became the proud parents of two little boys, Ernie and Charlie, and Eric became "Captain Eric Mosman," one of the few and the brave F4 Phantom fighter jet pilots.

But then early one morning in December 1984, Eric's squadron commander, accompanied by the base chaplain, knocked on their door. When Pammy heard the knock, she called out, "Come on in, Dave," expecting to see her next-door neighbor who was supposed to come over early to borrow a shovel. She looked up and saw the two officers instead.

"Oh," she said, "there's been an accident!" Military wives know that when the commanding officer and the chaplain appear at the front door with solemn faces, they're probably bringing very bad news.

"Yes, Pammy, it looks as if Eric is dead," the commanding officer said. And at that moment, the bottom fell out of Pammy's "perfect" world.

The same thing happened to Ruth, one of only two women in Scripture to have a whole book named after her. Like Pammy, Ruth became a young widow when her husband died.

> In the days when the judges ruled, there was a famine in the land, and a man from Bethlehem in Judah, together with his wife and two sons, went to live for a while in the country of Moab. The man's name was Elimelech, his wife's name Naomi, and the names of his two sons were Mahlon and Kilion. They were Ephrathites from Bethlehem, Judah. And they went to Moab and lived there.
> Now Elimelech, Naomi's husband died, and she was left with her two sons. They married Moabite women, one named Orpah and the other Ruth. After they had lived there about ten years, both Mahlon and Kilion also died, and Naomi was left without her two sons and her husband. (Ruth 1:1–5)

The Bible doesn't tell us what Ruth said when her husband died. We don't know if she was at his bedside when it happened or if someone knocked on the door to bring the bad news to her, as in Pammy's case. But Scripture does tell us what Ruth did when she found out that her husband was dead. Instead of returning to her mother's house and staying in her hometown of Moab, Ruth chose to leave all that was familiar and accompany her grieving mother-in-law back to Bethlehem.

As a matter of fact, the words we often hear quoted in marriage ceremonies are actually the words Ruth said to Naomi, after Naomi tried to convince her daughter-in-law to go on back home and find a nice man to marry: "Don't urge me to leave you or to turn back from you. Where you go I will go, and where you stay I will stay. Your people will be my people and your God my God. Where you die I will die, and there I will be buried. May the LORD deal with me, be it ever so severely, if anything but death separates you and me" (Ruth 1:16–17).

Sustaining Grace

What a wonderful picture of humble loyalty! Most young widows in Ruth's sandals would've run back home to Mama. They sure wouldn't have chosen to follow their miserable mother-in-law— who literally told people to start calling her *Mara,* which means "bitter"—back to a foreign land too far away for friends and family to visit. Ruth's faithfulness to Naomi was very unusual and very selfless given their circumstances.

That's probably why I'm reminded of Pammy now every time I read about Ruth. Pammy's faithfulness was also very unusual given her circumstances. When the commanding officer took hold of her forearms and told her that Eric was most likely dead, the first words out of her mouth were, "Oh, Colonel, right now my husband is beholding glory that you and I cannot imagine!"

The officer, who probably thought Pammy's response was her attempt to grasp for something hopeful, responded, "Yes, Pammy, I know Eric is in heaven, because he was a good man."

But Pammy, with tears streaming down her face, looked right into his eyes and replied, "Oh no, Colonel, Eric's in heaven because he knows Jesus."

And it was at that moment that Pammy turned around to see six-year-old Ernie and three-year-old Charlie standing behind her in their Superman "feety" pajamas. They had slipped down the hall in all the commotion and were quietly watching Pammy and the officers with tear-streaked faces. Pammy immediately took them both in her arms and walked to the living room. Sitting down with them on a large, overstuffed footstool, she said, "It looks as if the Lord has allowed Daddy to go to heaven. We won't see him any-more here, but we will see him again in heaven." And then God reminded her of a miracle of His providence, and she said, "Ernie, do you remember the Bible verse Daddy taught you last week and said with you last night?"

Little Ernie looked at her with a confused expression that said, *Oh, Mama, this is not the time for me to do my memory verses!* But then Pammy started to slowly recite the scripture that Eric had repeated with the boys just twelve hours earlier: "God is a..."

Ernie's blue eyes widened and his whole face lit up as he finished the verse his mommy started: "...a father to the fatherless and a hus-band to the husbandless" (Psalm 68:5, adapted).

And Pammy, widowed for less than an hour, explained to her

children the meaning of that scripture—that although it was very, very sad that Daddy was dead, God promised to take care of them. She pulled them even closer and prayed, "Lord, You tell us to give thanks in all things; and even though I don't feel like it, I thank You out of obedience and trust that You will work this out for the best for Charlie and Ernie and myself."

She lost her husband, her best friend, her lover, her children's father, their military housing, and her status as an officer's wife. "Yet," she said,

"NOTHING

could change the fact that I was a child of God."

It's been seventeen years since Pammy ministered the miraculous peace of God to her boys and those befuddled military officers. Ernie and Charlie are both godly young men now. They're in college, and Ernie is married to Jennifer, a precious Christian young woman. (No, they didn't meet under an oak tree!) And Pammy is even more of an example of God's grace now than she was then.

How have you responded when the bottom has fallen out of your world? Do you tend to doubt God's love when things go awry?

We were talking on the phone last night, and Pammy said that as horrible as Eric's death was, it ushered in the most powerful season of her life because she had to be utterly dependent on God. She said that during the weeks and months after Eric's plane went down, almost everything was stripped away from her. She lost her husband, her best friend, her lover, her children's father, their military housing, and her status as an officer's wife.

"Yet," she said, "nothing could change the fact that I was a child of God." She said that while she knew a lot of people thought that Romans 8:28 sounded trite and inappropriate during a tragedy— "And we know that in all things God works for the good of those who love him, who have been called according to his purpose"—it had given her great hope. "I stood on the promise of that verse," she said. "I knew that I knew that I knew that God was going to do something wonderful somehow."

The Wonderful Somehow

I wonder if that's what Ruth was thinking as she walked alongside Naomi back to Bethlehem. I wonder if she was anticipating a miracle when she began the tedious job of picking up leftover grain after the barley harvest so that she and Naomi could have something to eat. I wonder if she realized that she caught the eye of the kind landowner, Boaz, while she was working in his field. I wonder if she thought that something wonderful was about to happen when Boaz asked if she had a few minutes to talk.

> So Boaz said to Ruth, "My daughter, listen to me. Don't go and glean in another field and don't go away from here. Stay here with the servant girls. Watch the field where the men are harvesting, and follow along after the girls. I have told the men not to touch you. And whenever you are thirsty, go and get a drink from the water jars the men have filled."
>
> At this, she bowed down with her face to the ground. She exclaimed, "Why have I found such favor in your eyes that you notice me—a foreigner?"
>
> Boaz replied, "I've been told all about what you have done for your mother-in-law since the death of your husband—how you left your father and mother and your homeland and came to live with a people you did not know before. May the LORD

repay you for what you have done. May you be richly rewarded by the LORD, the God of Israel, under whose wings you have come to take refuge." (Ruth 2:8–12)

I bet Ruth had to pinch herself to make sure she wasn't dreaming! Here she was, the new girl in town and a widow to boot, and the biggest catch in Bethlehem had just confided that he had a crush on her! And it got even better. When Ruth rushed home to tell Naomi about Boaz, Naomi sat upright in her armchair, her old eyes widened, her face split into a grin, and she told Ruth something really exciting: "'The LORD bless him!' Naomi said to her daughter-in-law. 'He has not stopped showing his kindness to the living and the dead.' She added, 'That man is our close relative; he is one of our kinsman-redeemers'" (Ruth 2:20).

Based on Old Testament law, kinsman-redeemers could do three things: They could redeem a family member sold into slavery, they could redeem land that was sold by a family member under hardship, and they could redeem the family name by virtue of a levirate marriage. So the fact that Boaz was one of their kinsman-redeemers meant that he could legally buy Elimelech's estate, and he had the option of marrying Elimelech's daughter-in-law (Ruth) in order to keep the family lineage from dying out. No wonder Naomi's pessimism flew out the window and the twinkle returned to her eyes! She was transformed from "Mara the Bitter" to a matchmaking mother-in-law—and her matchmaking must've worked, because pretty soon Boaz dropped to one knee and asked Ruth to marry him. But more than Naomi's meddling, it was Ruth's humble faithfulness that led her down a barley-speckled aisle to a new life and a new love.

It would take another book to do justice to the rest of Pammy's story, but suffice it to say that God brought her a "Boaz," too. She met Jack Markle on November 4, 1985, and they got married on December 31 that same year—probably about the same short amount of time it took Boaz to sign the legal papers and pop the question to Ruth! Pammy and Jack had a sweet son (named John) a few years later. And, of course, so did Ruth and Boaz:

> So Boaz took Ruth and she became his wife. …And the LORD enabled her to conceive, and she gave birth to a son. The women said to Naomi: "Praise be to the LORD, who this day has not left you without a kinsman-redeemer. May he become famous throughout Israel! He will renew your life and sustain you in your old age. For your daughter-in-law, who loves you and who is better to you than seven sons, has given him birth."
>
> Then Naomi took the child, laid him in her lap and cared for him. The women living there said, "Naomi has a son." And they named him Obed. He was the father of Jesse, the father of David. (Ruth 4:13–17)

Two young widows with very similar stories. And both of their stories point to the compassion of a kinsman-redeemer. The God of Israel sent Ruth a kinsman-redeemer with skin on. His name was Boaz, and he was the providential owner of the place where she worked in Bethlehem. Boaz redeemed Ruth, and they got married and had a baby boy named Obed.

Twenty-nine generations later another baby boy—who was a direct descendant of Obed—was born. Also in the little town of Bethlehem. His mother delivered him in a cave, which could very well have been at the edge of one of the fields Ruth gathered grain in. His name was Jesus. He is the perfect Kinsman-Redeemer who sustained Pammy so many years later. His love is amazing. His mercies are sovereign. They are new every morning. Great is His faithfulness—even for those of us who aren't quite as faithful as the Ruths and Pammys of the world!

Focusing on His Faithfulness

1. Is there a "Pammy" in your life—someone who exemplifies trust in God, no matter what? Describe her or his trust.

_____

_____

_____

_____

_____

_____

2. Have you been able to thank God for _everything_ in your life? Why or why not?

_____

_____

_____

_____

_____

3. When you look back over the course of your life, can you see times when God created treasure out of tragedy? If so, how?

_____

_____

_____

_____

_____

_____

4. Rewrite Romans 8:28 in your own words. Looking back over your life, have there been any seasons where this verse *didn't* apply?

_____

_____

_____

_____

_____

_____

5. Read Psalm 103 out loud—really loud! Write here a "song" of praise for God's faithfulness to you. Go for a walk or a run or a drive and sing songs of praise.

_____

_____

_____

_____

_____

_____

_____

NOTES

chapter one

1. Frederick Buechner, *Peculiar Treasures* (New York: Harper-Collins, 1979), 47–48.

chapter two

1. C. S. Lewis, *A Grief Observed* (New York: Seabury Press, 1963), 79–81.

chapter six

1. J. Julius Scott, Jr., *Jewish Backgrounds of the New Testament* (Grand Rapids, Mich.: Baker Book House, 1995), 234–35.

2. W. E. Vine, Merrill F. Unger, and William White Jr., *Vine's Complete Expository Dictionary of Old and New Testament Words* (Nashville: Thomas Nelson, 1984, 1996), 316.

3. Scott, *Jewish Backgrounds of the New Testament*, 251–52.

chapter eight

1. Henri Nouwen, *The Inner Voice of Love* (New York: Random House, 1996), 84.

chapter nine

1. Nicole Johnson, *Dropping Your Rock* (n. p.: Nicole and Company Creative, n. d.), 46.

chapter ten

1. C. S. Lewis, *The Chronicles of Narnia: The Lion, the Witch and the Wardrobe* (New York: HarperCollins, 1978), 79–80.

chapter eleven

1. John Eldredge, *The Journey of Desire* (Nashville: Thomas Nelson, 2000), 54.

ABOUT
THE AUTHOR

LISA HARPER was the creator and hostess of Focus on the Family's Renewing the Heart Conferences, which involved almost 200,000 women. She is the author of *Every Woman's Hope*, the coauthor of *May Bell's Daughter* and *Renewed Hearts, Changed Lives*; and has contributed to several other books. She speaks at conferences and events around the country and directs the women's ministry at Christ Presbyterian in Nashville.

Breinigsville, PA USA
22 October 2009
226273BV00002B/12/A